AN INTRODUCTION TO AUTOMATED LITERATURE SEARCHING

BOOKS IN LIBRARY AND INFORMATION SCIENCE
A Series of Monographs and Textbooks
EDITOR
ALLEN KENT
Director, Office of Communications Programs
University of Pittsburgh
Pittsburgh, Pennsylvania

ADVISORY BOARD

C. David Batty
University of Maryland

Julie H. Bichteler
The University of Texas at Austin

Anindya Bose
University of Denver

Scott Bruntjen
Chatham College

Michael K. Buckland
University of California at Berkeley

Eric de Grolier
Paris, France

Tom Featheringham
New Jersey Institute of Technology

Maurice J. Freedman
Columbia University

Thomas J. Galvin
University of Pittsburgh

Edward J. Kazlauskas
University of Southern California

Chai Kim
State University of New York at Buffalo

Irving M. Klempner
State University of New York at Albany

Boaz Lazinger
Jerusalem, Israel

John A. McCrossan
University of South Florida

Paul E. Peters
Columbia University

Allan D. Pratt
The University of Arizona

Gary R. Purcell
The University of Tennessee

Tefko Saracevic
Case Western Reserve University

Thomas P. Slavens
The University of Michigan

Roy B. Stokes
The University of British Columbia

K. Subramanyam
Drexel University

Jean M. Tague
The University of Western Ontario

Vol. 1   Classified Library of Congress Subject Headings, Volume 1—Classified List, *edited by James G. Williams, Martha L. Manheimer, and Jay E. Daily* (out of print)
Vol. 2   Classified Library of Congress Subject Headings, Volume 2—Alphabetic List, *edited by James G. Williams, Martha L. Manheimer, and Jay E. Daily* (out of print)
Vol. 3   Organizing Nonprint Materials, *by Jay E. Daily*
Vol. 4   Computer-Based Chemical Information, *edited by Edward McC. Arnett and Allen Kent*
Vol. 5   Style Manual: A Guide for the Preparation of Reports and Dissertations, *by Martha L. Manheimer*
Vol. 6   The Anatomy of Censorship, *by Jay E. Daily*
Vol. 7   Information Science: Search for Identity, *edited by Anthony Debons* (out of print)
Vol. 8   Resource Sharing in Libraries: Why • How • When • Next Action Steps, *edited by Allen Kent* (out of print)
Vol. 9   Reading the Russian Language: A Guide for Librarians and Other Professionals, *by Rosalind Kent*
Vol. 10 Statewide Computing Systems: Coordinating Academic Computer Planning, *edited by Charles Mosmann* (out of print)
Vol. 11 Using the Chemical Literature: A Practical Guide, *by Henry M. Woodburn*
Vol. 12 Cataloging and Classification: A Workbook, *by Martha L. Manheimer* (out of print; see Vol. 30)
Vol. 13 Multi-media Indexes, Lists, and Review Sources: A Bibliographic Guide, *by Thomas L. Hart, Mary Alice Hunt, and Blanche Woolls*
Vol. 14 Document Retrieval Systems: Factors Affecting Search Time, *by K. Leon Montgomery*
Vol. 15 Library Automation Systems, *by Stephen R. Salmon*
Vol. 16 Black Literature Resources: Analysis and Organization, *by Doris H. Clack*
Vol. 17 Copyright—Information Technology—Public Policy: Part I—Copyright—Public Policies; Part II—Public Policies—Information Technology, *by Nicholas Henry*
Vol. 18 Crisis in Copyright, *by William Z. Nasri*
Vol. 19 Mental Health Information Systems: Design and Implementation, *by David J. Kupfer, Michael S. Levine, and John A. Nelson*
Vol. 20 Handbook of Library Regulations, *by Marcy Murphy and Claude J. Johns, Jr.* (out of print)
Vol. 21 Library Resource Sharing, *by Allen Kent and Thomas J. Galvin*
Vol. 22 Computers in Newspaper Publishing: User-Oriented Systems, *by Dineh Moghdam*
Vol. 23 The On-Line Revolution in Libraries, *edited by Allen Kent and Thomas J. Galvin*
Vol. 24 The Library as a Learning Service Center, *by Patrick R. Penland and Aleyamma Mathai*
Vol. 25 Using the Mathematical Literature: A Practical Guide, *by Barbara Kirsch Schaefer*
Vol. 26 Use of Library Materials: The University of Pittsburgh Study, *by Allen Kent et al.*
Vol. 27 The Structure and Governance of Library Networks, *edited by Allen Kent and Thomas J. Galvin*
Vol. 28 The Development of Library Collections of Sound Recordings, *by Frank W. Hoffmann*
Vol. 29 Furnishing the Library Interior, *by William S. Pierce*
Vol. 30 Cataloging and Classification: A Workbook Second Edition, Revised and Expanded, *by Martha L. Manheimer*

Vol. 31 Handbook of Computer-Aided Composition, *by Arthur H. Phillips*
Vol. 32 OCLC: Its Governance, Function, Financing, and Technology, *by Albert F. Maruskin*
Vol. 33 Scientific and Technical Information Resources, *by Krishna Subramanyam*
Vol. 34 An Author Index to Library of Congress Classification, Class P, Subclasses PN, PR, PS, PZ, General Literature, English and American Literature, Fiction in English, and Juvenile Belles Lettres, *by Alan M. Greenberg*
Vol. 35 Using the Biological Literature: A Practical Guide, *by Elisabeth B. Davis*
Vol. 36 An Introduction to Automated Literature Searching, *by Elizabeth P. Hartner*

Additional Volumes in Preparation

AN INTRODUCTION TO AUTOMATED LITERATURE SEARCHING

Elizabeth P. Hartner

MARCEL DEKKER, INC.　　　　　　　New York • Basel

Library of Congress Cataloging in Publication Data

Hartner, Elizabeth P., [date].
  An introduction to automated literature searching.

  (Books in library and information science ; v. 36)
  Includes index.
  1. Information retrieval. 2. Searching, Bibliographical--Automation. I. Title. II. Series.
  Z678.9.H33   025.5'24   81-7831
  ISBN 0-8247-1293-5   AACR2

COPYRIGHT © 1981 by MARCEL DEKKER, INC.   ALL RIGHTS RESERVED

Neither this book nor any part may be reproduced or transmitted in any form or by any means, electronic or mechanical, including photocopying, microfilming, and recording, or by any information storage and retrieval system, without permission in writing from the publisher.

MARCEL DEKKER, INC.
270 Madison Avenue, New York, New York 10016

Current printing (last digit):
10 9 8 7 6 5 4 3 2

PRINTED IN THE UNITED STATES OF AMERICA

Preface

John Masefield, in his book <u>So Long to Learn</u>, wrote about his experience in the British Museum reading room:

> In a few days I began to learn how to look for subjects; I came to know the arrangements, the Indices and Catalogues, the multitudes of helps to knowledge. I obtained entry to what was called the Large Room, which was so much quieter than the Rotunda. I went sometimes to the Manuscript Room; and then, later, to the Record Office. Soon, I knew fairly well how to pursue a subject, and deeply knew the joy of the chase. Often, the excitement of the chase kept me awake at night, with the problem of what to examine next. I had decided that <u>all</u> the past is buried in those collections, and could be found by resolute search. It is not so. Time has destroyed a good deal and well-hidden a great deal more. The seeker cannot always find, even after days of trouble. If the search daily revealed my great ignorance, it daily shewed me how the ignorance might be lessened. Sometimes, I had the unexpected bliss of finding just what I wanted or had hoped-for.[*]

It is John Masefield's "joy of the chase" that motivates the seeker of information. The enthusiast will use all means available. Sometime after the expansion of computer methods for handling large quantities of data during World War II, it became apparent that computer methods of sifting through thousands of documents could be used to find published information.

This book is an introduction to the practical side of performing computer searches of scientific and technical literature. It is written for neophytes in the automated retrieval of published literature, whether they be a research scientist, technical problem solver, science writer, technical librarian, or college beginner. While the lists of references for each chapter are not the result of exhaustive literature searches, they may start the reader along a path which will take him as far into the technology and theory as he wants to go.

---

[*] Reproduced with permission from Macmillan Publishing Company, <u>So Long to Learn</u> by John Masefield (copyright 1952 by John Masefield).

Preface

To perform the introduction to automated literature searching, the basic methods of finding information are first considered (Chapter 1); what sources are available for automated literature searching (Chapter 2); methods of automated searching (Chapter 3); and how the results of automated searching can be presented (Chapter 4). Further helps to understanding are how the results can be judged (Chapter 5); and an explanation of how the computer processes a search (Chapter 6). The reader who knows little about computer processing may find it helpful to read Chapter 6 before reading Chapters 2 and 3.

Since writing the book, I have noted many changes in the fast-moving field of automated literature searching. The commercial online data services have become a major industry. Many of the characteristics of the files have been improved, and many new data bases developed. An example of a change is that the file Metadex, discussed in Chapter 2, now has abstracts available for printing and searching. The Chemical Abstracts Service has made the CAS Chemical Registry System structure file searchable online. The search programs and formatting of requests for the various online services are not discussed in the book because of the continual format modifications to make the application of Boolean logic easier as well as the combination of different fields and sequences. All such approaches are best learned when the user is ready to start active searching, or are best left to an intermediary information scientist if the user prefers.

I am indebted to many colleagues from the Knowledge Availability Systems Center, the University of Pittsburgh, over the years 1965-1975, who have assisted directly and indirectly in the preparation of this book. I particularly wish to thank Professor Allen Kent, Distinguished Service Professor, School of Library and Information Science, the University of Pittsburgh, for his advice as to the order of the chapters, valuable criticisms of the manuscript, and encouragement.

I also wish to thank Professor James G. Williams of the University of Pittsburgh, Mary Marshall, Carolyn and Karl Hartner, and my husband Howard E. Hartner for reading and commenting on parts of the manuscript. Other University of Pittsburgh staff members, including Priscilla Mercier and Professor Eleanor Dym have my gratitude for their support of my efforts. My sister, Jocelyn Harrington, has my heartfelt thanks for substituting her good right hand for my broken one in early 1981. And the same thanks go to Mary Marshall for her help in reading proof.

Elizabeth P. Hartner

Contents

Preface iii

chapter 1 / HOW DO YOU FIND INFORMATION? 1

    Introduction 1
    Identifying the Information Need 3
    Sources of Information 5
    How This Book Will be Limited 7
    Summary 9
    Appendix: Partial List of Information
        Science Journals 9
    References 11

chapter 2 / FILES AVAILABLE FOR MECHANIZED RETRIEVAL ... 13

    Introduction 13
    The Information Explosion and Overlap 13
    Government Files 22
    Files Produced by Societies and Organizations 22
    Academic Files 23
    Commercially Produced Files 25
    Summary 27
    Appendix: Some Files Available for Subjects
        in Science and Technology 27
    References 29

chapter 3 / THE STRATEGY OF MECHANIZED SEARCH ... 31

    Introduction 31
    Entry Points 31
    Searching by Boolean Logic 52
    Weighting 59
    The Use of Postings in Strategy Building 60
    Effect of Recall and Precision on Strategy Building . 62
    Summary 63

Appendix I: Searching Work Flow	63
Appendix II: Example of Search Procedures and Results	64
References	66

chapter 4 / PRESENTATION OF SEARCH RESULTS 68

Introduction	68
Products of Mechanized Retrieval	69
Bibliographies	74
Bibliographies with Abstracts	80
Annotated Bibliographies	80
Structured Reference Listings	80
Digests and Reviews	82
Reports	82
Special Files	83
Summary	84
Appendix I: Example of a Categorized Bibliography	84
Appendix II: Example of a Digest	88
Appendix III: Example of Report of Literature Review	89
References	90

chapter 5 / JUDGING THE RESULTS OF MECHANIZED RETRIEVAL 92

Introduction	92
How Do You Know the Search Was Effective?	92
When the User Finds the Results Unsatisfactory	102
Summary	103
Appendix I: Example of Indexing Inaccuracies	103
Appendix II: A Flow Diagram for Current Awareness	104
References	104

chapter 6 / HOW COMPUTERIZED RETRIEVAL WORKS 106

Introduction: Use of the Computer for Mechanized Retrieval	106
How Information is Stored for Electronic Access	107
How Information is Retrieved	118
Summary	123
References	123

Glossary	125
Index	137

AN INTRODUCTION TO AUTOMATED LITERATURE SEARCHING

chapter 1
How Do You Find Information?

INTRODUCTION

Information is a basic need. The spider must know where insects often fly before it spins its web. The human must know where stairs are before going to the next level. For every bit of information there can be many sources. Where the stairs are is information which may come from the observing eye. If one is blind or in the dark, information may come from a probing hand or foot. A descriptive floor plan may tell the visitor where to look for stairs in a strange building.

In this book we will be considering graphical sources of information, such as a floor plan. Graphical sources may be drawings or diagrams, or printed books, magazines, journals, reports, and newspapers. Civilized mankind has stored graphical information on stone, on papyrus rolls, in books, on film, in computer memory, etc. This book is addressed to the techniques of finding information by computer processing.

The act of publishing indicates that the information published may be of interest to someone, somewhere, at some time. For this reason publications are stored in libraries of books, on microfilm rolls and aperture cards, on magnetic tapes or disks, or directly in core computer memory. Published information must be stored so that it can be found. In a library, books can be shelved with a unique number for each book. Each shelf may be identified by a subject area alphanumeric code which is included in the book number. The individual book may then be easily found and easily returned to the shelf.

If the information is placed on microfilm rolls or aperture cards, it can be stored much as library books are stored, and located by means of labels. On the other hand the microfilm or aperture cards may bear coded identifications allowing the information to be located by a mechanized film reader. Such automated devices, although often electronically programmed to perform their tasks, usually depend on an item number or a code such as chapter and page rather than on item surrogates consisting of identifying alphabetics.

Items on magnetic tapes or disks which are mounted for electronic reading by a computer, and items stored in primary (core) computer memory, can also be indexed or coded and stored in subsets by subject categories, year of publication, author, and other methods for "shelving." The computer is programmed to examine each item for requested identifying surrogates such as an author's name, an author's name and a year of publication, a descriptive word such as the name of a chemical compound, or a list of words meaningful in the context of the inquiry. So rapidly does the computer perform the search that an examination of even a large file, which might be the equivalent of a large specialized library, may take less than a minute. Most computer searchable files are therefore listings of items in random order, which neatly avoids the error resulting from an item being "misshelved"—incorrectly located within the file. It should be remembered, however, that each file is finite. Therefore an item may be "misshelved" in that it is not included in what appears to be the appropriate file. Also, there is no guarantee, at present at least, that every published item will appear on an automated file of some kind.

Although much that is published is useless or repetitive, there is no way to know in advance what is unworthy or redundant. What is unworthy to one may be worthy to another. Scientific journals rely on peer review to prevent the publication of useless material, but peer opinion has sometimes failed to recognize an unorthodox or unconventional paper as a major contribution to science. An example of such a paper is Darwin's original "On the Tendency of Species to Form Varieties, and on the Perpetuation of Varieties and Species by Natural Means of Selection."

Repetitive publishing of papers can be discouraging, as when three out of five references uncovered by a search turn out to be identical. Nevertheless little time or money is spent to eliminate duplicates. Duplicate papers insure that the item will be more easily found, although that is weak justification. We can only hope that the item is worth finding.

The growth in the annual production of published information is so great that it is impossible for a scientist to read all that is published, even in a comparatively narrow field of interest. The publications in science, technology, and engineering constitute an enormous sea in which only the most sophisticated fishing tackle will enable searchers to find what they seek.

When a search for information is begun, the new user may find many applicable files. In time, if he searches often, particularly in one subject area, he finds a limited number, or even only one, that he feels gives the most reliable results. However, sometimes information known to exist may prove difficult to find, and many files may have to be searched.

While this book is about automated information retrieval, it should be emphasized that the automated portion of a search is simply a computer-using method for sifting and sorting large amounts of information. A preliminary manual investigation and study will give needed direction to the automated search. For trained users of automated retrieval, the manual preparation may be no more than ten to fifteen minutes of thought, but it is always worthwhile.

IDENTIFYING THE INFORMATION NEED

Kinds of Information Needs

Information needs can take several forms. The need may be a "look-up." For instance, one may need to know the population of Dade County, Florida; or the molecular formula of saccharin; or the melting point of AISI 436 steel.

The need may, on the other hand, be for the answer to a question more complicated than a simple look-up. It might be "How many of the population of Dade County, Florida, were born in Dade County between the years 1970 and 1975?" or "What metals and alloys have melting points between 150 and 200° C?" or "What organic acids with the basic structure of acetic acid contain the phenyl radical?"

Problems of various kinds also require information retrieval for solution. Examples might be "A new grade school is to be built in Dade County, to be completed by 1980. How many students can be expected for grades 1 through 6 in the decade after 1980?" or "A low-melting alloy, electrically conducting, not corrodable, and nonpoisonous, is needed for a certain application." or "Can you find in the chemical literature any evidence of a sweet-tasting compound which could be used as a sugar substitute with no adverse effects on humans?"

The fourth kind of information need is for background or state-of-the-art information—the sort required to write an article or book, or to begin a new scientific or engineering project. The background information needed may be for an understanding of the field in general, in which case a few good recent articles or reviews will fill the need. Alternatively, an exhaustive coverage may be required, for example to insure that a proposed doctoral thesis will be original research.

User needs will vary from organization to organization. When a unit of an organization, such as a library, is proposing to make automated literature searching available to organization members, a study should be made of files, commercial services, and internal organization information systems, in order to determine the best way to supply what the organization users need [1].

Methods of Expressing the Information Need

When a searcher—whether the ultimate user of the information or a professional hired by the user to make the search—begins a search, the first step should be to write a description of the required information. The act of putting the words down on paper will clarify the user's needs both to the user and to the searcher. In addition, if the words describing the interest are found by the computer to occur in the title, index terms, or abstract of a file item, the item can be considered to be of possible interest to the user. The more words and synonyms specific to the interest that are identified, the smaller will be the mesh of the "fishing net," and the more effective will it be. Such descriptive words are called <u>keywords</u>.

As an example of a real-life need for information, the user might say "I would like to get some information about the treatment of various kinds of waste water." When asked to write a description of the interest, the user might prepare the following: "In studies of the pollution of streams in the vicinity of _____, we have found that although most of the industries and towns have begun to treat their waste water, there is still a difference between unpolluted streams and streams that receive runoff of some kind from industries and towns that treat their waste water. We are interested in the methods of treating waste water, in whether some methods are better than others, and in what the chemical products of the treatments are."

When the search is performed by a professional literature searching organization, the user is interviewed by a searcher who has a background in the subject of the user's interest, who is familiar with the files available in the subject area, and who is experienced in manipulating the search program capabilities. An in-depth knowledge of the specific subject field, while advantageous, is not necessary if the professional searcher has sufficient general knowledge to ask the user penetrating or leading questions. In fact, insufficient knowledge on the part of the interviewer may produce questions that inspire the user to give a detailed and enthusiastic description of the whole background of the question, thus revealing keywords which the searcher may find useful. Nothing is easier than to lead a scientist or engineer to talk at length about his enthusiasm of the moment.

The searcher for the above question on waste water treatment would certainly ask whether the user had anything specific in mind in regard to the chemical products of waste water treatment. He would also ask, among other things, whether effects of changes in temperature or weather on amount of stream pollution would be of interest.

The user should also give the searcher supplementary helpful material such as titles of publications which might contain relevant information. Any applicable terminology used in the particular subject field, but not commonly known outside it, should also be provided. For the waste water problem, the user might provide titles such as:

Industrial Sanitation and Treatment of Waste Waters in the Meat Industry
Purification and Disinfection of Waste Waters from Hospitals

Manual for Chemical Analysis of Inland Waters
Optimum Feed Rate of a Coagulant During Water Treatment

Note how the titles selected by the user as promising have brought new terms to the attention of the searcher: sanitation, purification, disinfection, hospitals, inland waters, coagulant.

The final search statement prepared for the guidance of the searcher might go something like this: "The interest is in the treatment, purification, disinfection, and sanitation of waste waters from industries, town sanitary systems, and hospitals. We would like to know what are the products of treatment, whatever the nature of the treatment—chemical reaction of the wastes to form soluble nontoxic substances, or the formation of insoluble materials such as sludges by coagulation." The searcher has included in the statement all potentially valuable keywords for future guidance.

SOURCES OF INFORMATION

Authorities in the Field

After the information need has been identified, discussed, and clarified, a plan must be made as to where to go for the information. The source to which scientists and engineers usually turn first is a known authority. The easiest and most natural thing to do is to call a colleague, a former professor, or any other associate who might have more knowledge of the subject of interest than oneself.

The authority in the field may offer historical recollection. "John Smith published a comprehensive resumé on the subject in 1956." Or the authority may have a recipe or set of instructions at his fingertips. "The most successful welds that we have made of the sheet steel that you are using for your sculpture have been by using E70S-G welding wire in an inert gas atmosphere." "The Covered Wagon Chemical Company has put out a booklet No. 3829 about methods of applying the rust preventive paint Dinosaur Pelt which they have developed. It is good stuff and would probably work fine on your porch railings."

Sometimes the authority can supply enough data to answer the information need. For example, the expert might be able to say "We have been interviewing freshman college students and have data about their precollege skills. The results so far indicate that less than 25% of incoming students can type. Typing instruction would therefore be a good precollege summer session subject to offer at your university."

It is of importance to remember that the name of the known authority (as an author) may be used as a search term for automated retrieval.

How Do You Find Information?

Reference Books

Reference books will provide the answer to many information needs. The first approach is to examine the catalogs of available libraries whose holdings cover the subject area of interest. Entering the card catalog of a large technical library by subject or author will lead the searcher to reference and text books which will provide information. In addition, the card catalog will identify the Dewey decimal numbers or Library of Congress numbers by which the user's subject of interest is labeled in the library, and thus permit browsing the shelves, a most rewarding occupation. For instance, the identifying alphanumerics for Geology are QE in the LC classification, and 550 in the Dewey decimal classification. A narrower subdivision of geology will be identified by alphanumerics beginning with QE for the LC and 550 for the Dewey classification.

Histories of the subject may contain leads to valuable information which may have been buried or forgotten. From history comes the information that early craftsmen used "gold wash" to preserve objects from atmospheric attack. Nowadays precious metal films may be applied by electrolytic deposition or vacuum deposition. A modern term which has been applied to the craft is "flashing."

Sometimes a subject may appear to be so narrow as to make it difficult to locate information. If one is lucky, a monograph or textbook will exist that presents between two covers all there is to know on the subject. When a large subject area, such as polymer chemistry, is the specialization field of an information organization, current awareness surveys of newly published books and monographs in that subject area are important. Coverage of a suitable abstract index such as Chemical Abstracts on a regular monthly basis will help to keep the organization aware of new books. For instance, Chemical Abstracts, Volume 83 (1975), issue 18, section 61, abstract number 152131 gives the information that a 42 page book Canadian Drinking Water Standards and Objectives, a second edition, has been written by the Joint Committee on Drinking Water Standards, Canada, and published by Inform, Canada, in Ottawa, Ontario.

Frequently, catalogs of data published by individual companies or trade associations are valuable reference material. For instance the National Micrographics Association, 8728 Colesville Road, Silver Spring, MD 20910, publishes A Microform Handbook and an Introduction to Micrographics for those interested in the subject of micropublishing. Many chemical companies, such as Eastman, DuPont, and Pennwalt, will supply descriptive literature of their products upon request.

Published Articles, Reports, Summaries

By far the most used sources of information in the technical, engineering, and scientific fields are published articles, reports, and summaries. When

How This Book Will Be Limited   7

the user is interested in the latest findings, made since the publication of
the basic reference books, recent publication in journals and recent reports
are the best resources. For complete confidence in the coverage of a subject it is always necessary to see what has appeared in print up to date.
   Abstract journals continuously monitor journals relevant to their subject areas. The relevant articles, classified and abstracted in the abstract
journals, are usually the first source to which one turns in preparing lists
of articles on a given subject. Some of the leading abstract journals in the
fields of science and engineering are:

> Chemical Abstracts, published by Chemical Abstracts Service
> Engineering Index, published by Engineering Index, Inc.
> Science Abstracts, published by the Institute of Electrical Engineers
> Scientific and Technical Aerospace Reports, published by the National
>   Aeronautics and Space Administration
> Sociological Abstracts, published by Sociological Abstracts, Inc.

All of these abstract journals are available at the present time for automated retrieval.
   Abstract journals will run on the average three to six months behind
the appearance of the original article. To bring a subject completely up to
date it is necessary to examine the recent tables of contents and indexes of
the technical journals in the subject area. As an example of the number of
published journals in one technical field, Appendix I derived from reference
[2], lists journals from which reference papers were taken for two review
articles in the field of information science.

HOW THIS BOOK WILL BE LIMITED

To Technical Information

Information seeking is certainly not confined to the field of science and
engineering. Physics, chemistry, and astronomy are among those known
as "hard" sciences, because verifiable precision is possible. But the
meetings of the American Association for the Advancement of Science also
include sessions on sociology, anthropology, and economic and political
science, where conclusions may be based on statistics. Technical information can therefore be considered to include the social sciences. In the
last fifty years, the amount of technical publication has grown so rapidly
that it is an overwhelming task to do a good literature search in the library.
An examination of the section headings for the eighty sections into which
the abstracts in the bimonthly Chemical Abstracts are classified shows the
great number of major specializations recognized in the field of chemistry.
Publications appear in all of these fields of specialization.

In addition to publications in pure science and engineering, publications concerning world markets and education are examples of contiguous fields that yield information of value to certain technical subjects.

This book will be limited to methods of searching the literature of pure science, including the social sciences, engineering, markets, and education.

Limitation to Mechanically Stored and Retrievable Information

As discussed above, automated information consists of tapes, disks, or other memory devices, on which identifying surrogates for published information are stored. The surrogates usually consist of author names, article titles, journal references where the articles may be found, index terms, and sometimes an abstract of the article. Very few files contain the full article. An increasing number of nonbibliographic data files, in which data has been culled from various sources and organized, are becoming available. Many of these are searchable by computer and are utilized for technical searches.

The information on automated files may be obtained by purchasing or leasing the tapes from the file producer and purchasing or developing a computer program to search them. Large companies such as DuPont, Eastman Kodak, and the Bell Laboratories have found such an approach advantageous. They are able to merge the search results from the purchased or leased tapes with the results of their own internal information system.

In the last five years the use of commercial online access has grown tremendously. Lockheed, System Development Corporation, New York Times Information Bank, Mead Data Central, Dow-Jones News/Retrieval, and Bibliographic Retrieval Services are examples of commercial online information retrieval companies which make the information stored in their computers available to users throughout the world for a fee based on the cost of minutes online, of offline printout of results, and of communication. It is necessary to rent or own a computer terminal capable both of receiving coded information sent over the telephone and of sending out over the telephone coded instructions to the computer.

Specialized information centers, such as the NASA Industrial Application Centers [3], the University of Georgia Information Center, and the Illinois Institute of Technology Research Institute, and online organizations such as the System Development Corporation, acquire tapes from tape producers such as Engineering Index, Chemical Abstracts Service, and the Institute of Scientific Information. The service offered from processing the tapes varies from a list of references to an evaluated bibliography.

More sophisticated information centers do more than provide a list of selected references. These centers provide output in various forms ranging

Appendix

from bibliographies, to abstract bulletins, to evaluated information reports. An example of an organization which will provide critical surveys is the Metals and Ceramic Information Center (MCIC) of Battelle Memorial Institute. Selected subject bibliographies on a current awareness basis (updated at specified time intervals) are also prepared by several producers such as NASA (SCAN) [4] and Chemical Abstracts Services (CA SELECTS).

This book will be limited to automated searches of purchased or leased tapes, or of commercial online services.

SUMMARY

To find information it is necessary first to identify the exact information need. Sources of information include primary journals, data handbooks, textbooks and monographs, abstract journals, libraries, and automated information retrieval systems. This book will consider the retrieval of mechanically stored and retrievable technical information.

APPENDIX   Partial List of Information Science Journals

Name of journal	Number of references
Advances in Librarianship	1
American Education	1
American Psychologist	1
ASLIB Proceedings	9
Australian Library Journal	1
Bookmark	2
Bulletin ASIS	1
Bulletin of the Medical Library Association	8
California Librarian	3
Canadian Library Journal	1
College and Research Libraries	8
Communications of the ACM	2
Comparative Political Studies	1

APPENDIX (continued)

Name of journal	Number of references
Computers and Biomedical Research	1
Data Management	2
Drexel Library Quarterly	1
FID New Bulletin	1
Harvard Librarian	1
IBM Journal of Research and Development	1
Illinois Libraries	1
Information Retrieval and Library Automation	1
Information Storage and Retrieval	19
Interfaces	1
Japan Electronic Engineering	1
Journal of Chemical Information and Computer Sciences (formerly, Journal of Chemical Documentation)	22
Journal of Documentation	14
Journal of Librarianship	5
Journal of Library Automation	8
Journal of Marketing	1
Journal of Micrographics	1
Journal of Research and Development in Education	1
Journal of Systems Management	1
Journal of the American Society for Information Science	15
Library Association Record	1
Library Journal	2

References

APPENDIX (continued)

Name of journal	Number of references
Library Quarterly	2
Library Resources and Technical Services	5
Library Trends	3
Microform Review	2
Modern Data	1
Nachrichten für Dokumentation	1
NASPA Journal	1
OCLC Newsletter	1
OSTI Newsletter	1
Program	4
Public Administration Review	2
Public Opinion Quarterly	1
Rural Sociology	1
Special Libraries	7
Teacher's College Record	1
UNESCO Bulletin for Libraries	4
Wisconsin Library Bulletin	1

Source: As derived from two review papers from Ref. 2.

REFERENCES

1. A. C. Jones, "Presenting a Development Plan for Approval." In AGARD Conference Proceedings No. 117 Information in Industry and Simple Mechanization for Small Information Centers. Presented at the 25th meeting of the AGARD Technical Information Panel at the State Institute of Statistics, Ankara, Turkey, Oct. 23-24, 1972. North Atlantic Treaty Organization, Advisory Group for Aerospace Research and Development.

2. Carlos A. Cuadro and Ann W. Luke. Annu. Rev. Inf. Sci. Technol. 10, 1975.
3. National Aeronautics and Space Administration, Scientific and Technical Information Division, Office of Technology Utilization. "The NASA Scientific and Technical Information System—and How to Use It." Washington, D. C., 1970.
4. V. A. Wente and G. A. Young. "Selective Information Announcement Systems for a Large Community of Users." J. Chem. Document. 7, August 1967, 142.

chapter 2

Files Available for Mechanized Retrieval

THE INFORMATION EXPLOSION AND OVERLAP

Introduction

When it has been determined that an automated search is in order, that is, when the information need has been identified and the probable sources narrowed down to published articles, reports, or summaries, a decision must be made as to what file or files will yield relevant information.
The Appendix (page 27) lists the files mentioned in this chapter. For more complete coverage of available files the reader is referred to [1]. While available files are, for the most part, bibliographic files, nonbibliographic data files are becoming more available and may often prove useful. A directory of nonbibliographic data bases has been prepared by the Library of Congress [2].
 The "information explosion" of published science and technology since World War II makes the selection of the right files increasingly difficult. A request for recent literature in the field of electrical engineering may lead the searcher to consider a number of bibliographic files such as NTIS (National Technical Information Service), COMPENDEX (Computerized Engineering Index), INSPEC (International Information Services in Physics, Electrotechnology, Computers and Control), WAA (World Aluminum Abstracts), METADEX (Metals Abstracts Index), and others. Of course, the searcher is aware that each of the journals that contain publications in the field of electrical engineering may be covered by several of these files. In other words, there is overlap in coverage from one file to another. Yet each file is limited in size, and no file covers _all_ potentially useful information. As a matter of fact, very few files abstract cover to cover the journals which they examine. Usually the file editors select papers to be included from each of the journals examined.
 Very few studies of overlap have been made. A study of overlap in journal coverage by CACON, BIOSIS, and COMPENDEX [3] indicated that

of 14,592 journals covered, only 1% were covered by all three, 27% by two out of the three, and 72% were covered by only one of the files. Since the orientations of the files differ, these results are not unexpected. More informative would be a study of overlap in coverage for specific searches of various files. Results of unpublished studies by the author are shown in Tables 2.1 and 2.2. Table 2.1 gives the results from a general search on the subject of the corrosion of titanium, using the three files METADEX, CACON, and NASA. Of the 111 relevant references identified, only one appeared in all three files. Seven appeared in both METADEX and CACON, four in METADEX and NASA, and three in CACON and NASA. If METADEX had been the only file searched, 54% of the relevant references would have been found. Since titanium corrosion is a chemical process, the addition of a CACON search netted 37% more of the relevant abstracts. Because of the importance of titanium to the aeronautical industry, a search of the NASA file uncovered 9% more of the total number of citations found. It should be noted that this 100% does not represent the total universe of relevant documents.

Table 2.2 gives the results from a specific question about stress analysis. Of the 74 relevant references identified, only one appeared in all three files. One reference appeared in both CACON and METADEX; four references appeared in both NASA and METADEX; and two references appeared in both NASA and CACON. A search of METADEX would have

TABLE 2.1 Numbers of References Resulting from Search on the Subject of Corrosion Resistance of Titanium

Abstract file	Abstract file			
	METADEX	CACON	NASA	Total
METADEX	48	7	4	59
CACON	7	38	3	48
NASA	4	3	10	17
Total	59	48	17	—

Hits on all three files: 1

Total no. unique documents: 111

METADEX: 54%

CACON: 44%

NASA: 16%

TABLE 2.2 Numbers of References Resulting from Search on the Subject of Stress Analysis

Abstract file	Abstract file			
	METADEX	CACON	NASA	Total
METADEX	36	1	4	41
CACON	1	8	2	11
NASA	4	2	22	28
Total	41	11	28	—

Hits on all three files: 1

Total no. unique documents: 74

METADEX: 57%

CACON: 16%

NASA: 39%

uncovered 57% of the relevant abstracts. Since the question is in the area of deformation, a wise choice of a second file would be NASA, which would have yielded 32% more of the relevant abstracts.

With such results from literature searches, and with the growing availability of automated files, decisions about which files to search must be governed by the amount of information in each file, the subject fields covered by each file, and experience in searching each file.

Amount of Information in Machine Searchable Form

A number of listings of machine searchable files are available. One of the best is the directory published and updated by the American Society for Information Science [1]. As originally issued in 1976, this publication covered 277 data bases. At that time, 107 of the data bases were known to be processed online. Since 1976 new data bases have been made available for automated processing every year; and the number of files searchable online by the subscriber interacting through a communications link with the provider's computer has steadily increased. As of the end of 1978, two commercial providers of online searching were the System Development Corporation (SDC), with 51 files available, and Lockheed, with 94. In 1976, 52 million records were available for automated searching. Of these, 33 million were on line.

The size of a file—the number of records in it—varies considerably. A given file may be small but may yield for a specific subject area references not found in other files. Oppenheim and Sutherland [4], studying the coverage of nonpatent literature on GALVALUME by abstract journals, demonstrated the occurrence of additional references in the small specific abstract journals such as Centre Technique de Zinc, Bulletin Analytique. Table 2.3 is a table taken from Ref. 4. Were each of the abstract journals shown in Table 2.3 an automated file, Metals Abstracts (METADEX) and World Aluminum Abstracts (WAA) would be the two which would yield 40% of the relevant articles. The next choice would be Centre Technique du Zinc, Bulletin Analytique with 30% more.

TABLE 2.3 Coverage of Nonpatent Liberature on GALVALUME by Abstract Journals[a]

Article	Abstract journal[a]									
	1	2	3	4	5	6	7	8	9	10
a	—	—	—	—	X	X	—	X	—	—
b	—	—	—	—	—	X	—	X	—	—
c	X	—	—	—	—	—	—	—	—	X
d	X	—	—	—	—	—	—	—	—	—
e	—	—	—	—	—	X	—	X	—	—
f	—	—	—	—	X	—	X	—	—	—
g	—	—	X	—	—	—	—	—	—	—
h	—	—	X	—	—	—	—	—	—	—
j	—	—	—	—	—	X	—	X	—	—
k	—	—	X	—	—	—	—	—	—	—
Total	2	0	3	0	2	4	1	4	0	1

[a]Key to articles is given in Table V. Key to journals: (1) BNF Abs., (2) Bulletin Signaletique, (3) Centre Technique du Zinc, Bulletin Analytique, (4) Chemical Abstracts, (5) Metal Finishing Abstracts, (6) World Aluminum Abstracts, (7) Zinc Abstracts, (8) Metals Abstracts, (9) British Technology Index, (10) Applied Science and Technology Index.
Source: Reprinted with permission from Table VI, Oppenheim, C. and Sutherland, E. A., Studies on metallurgical patent literature, I., J. Chem. Inf. Comput. Sci., 18, no. 3, p. 128. Copyright by the American Chemical Society (1978).

The Information Explosion and Overlap

Three of these abstract journals have automated duplicates. The largest file is the Chemical Abstracts file (CACON) which has approximately 3,394,000 citations. Next is Metals Abstracts (METADEX), with approximately 390,000 citations. The smallest is World Aluminum Abstracts (WAA) with about 58,000 citations. From Table 2.3 (for nonpatent literature), the largest file does not seem to be the best choice for the search in question, even though this search is chemically oriented. The authors make the point, however, that for this and similar new-process searches, information may be contained in the patent literature, which Chemical Abstracts covers well in the chemical field. A search of the patent literature [4] found Chemical Abstracts identifying by far the greatest number of citations.

File size should be considered in selecting files to search. METADEX, limited to metallurgy, is a comparatively small file (390,000 records). Many metallurgical searches will be more successful if supplemented by CACON (3,394,000 records), NASA (STAR and IAA) (953,000 records), or COMPENDEX (751,000 records), as demonstrated by the data in Tables 2.1 and 2.2.

Subject Fields Covered by Machine Searchable Files

In view of the large number of science and technology files available, it is obvious that to search for information on a specified subject one must select the file or files most apt to yield a comprehensive coverage of the required information. As a first approach one could examine the subject index of The Directory of Computer Readable Data Bases [1]. The data bases in this source are listed under wide general subjects. For instance, 116 data bases are listed under "Chemistry and Chemical Engineering," with four "see also" subjects. "Materials Science" is not a heading. "Business, Economics and Management" has 64 files and one "see also" reference. "Philosophy" has 15 listed files.

More specific, but still quite general, listings are used by the Lockheed-Dialog subject guide [5]. Under "Chemistry," 21 data bases are suggested. The term "Materials Science" has 16 listings. "Business" has 21 listings, and "Philosophy" 5. In December 1978, the SDC Search Service announced an online index for selecting the best data bases for a search. To use this index, one enters search terms online and obtains a ranked listing of the data bases best suited to the search, based on the number of entries (postings) to each of the subject terms in each of the data bases. Combinations of terms can also be studied.

Another listing, with fewer suggested files, has been presented by Teitelbaum and Hawkins [6] of the Bell Laboratories. In this listing, one file (Chemical Abstracts) is suggested for the unmodified term "Chemistry," with the suggestion of more specific files such as METADEX or PAPERCHEM. For "Materials Science," four files are suggested, for "Business (General)," six files, and for "Philosophy," one file.

Special information science books or articles which are subject-oriented will often be of great help. Examples of these are [7—10]. The magazine Online has published a number of expert discussions of files available in different disciplines, for instance [11] for business information.

Often, a good approach to selecting files for searching a specific subject is to examine the journal coverage of the files. If the file covers the journals in which relevant articles have appeared, then the file should be searched. Graeme Hirst [12] describes a method for determining core journals for a discipline, using Journal Citation Reports. The method could be adapted for the selection of automated files by examining the journal sources of articles cited by a relevant paper.

Table 2.4, from an unpublished study by the author, shows the references selected as relevant to a question in the field of process metallurgy. Three files were covered: COMPENDEX, CACON, and METADEX. The printout from the COMPENDEX file included abstracts; the CACON printout gave author affiliations but not abstracts; and the METADEX printout gave neither abstracts nor author affiliations. For citations appearing on two or three files, therefore, the most useful reference was the one from COMPENDEX, and the next best the one from CACON. If a citation is in COMPENDEX or CACON, that does not necessarily mean that it is not in the METADEX file. Indexing (deeper on COMPENDEX than on the other two files) and editorial selection do, however, play a part. Very few duplicates of citations identified on the CACON or COMPENDEX files were found in the METADEX file.

All the journals listed (by CODEN) in Table 2.4 are so strongly metallurgical that they are certain to have been covered by METADEX. In other words, none of the journals listed could conceivably be covered by COMPENDEX or CACON alone. ISIPBU is the CODEN for Iron and Steel Institute, London. Coverage of COMPENDEX alone would have missed six references, and of CACON alone, five references. If METADEX were not covered, two references from AREIAT (Archiv für Eisenhuttenwesen) would be missed. Although REMEAH (Revue de Metallurgie) and STEIA3 (Stahl und Eisen) are covered to some extent by COMPENDEX and CACON, apparently the indexing or editorial selection must be such that the relevant items from those journals were not found in the COMPENDEX or CACON files.

From the data available it is not possible to say that coverage of the METADEX file would have resulted in the retrieval of all the relevant papers found. What can be said is that the use of either COMPENDEX or CACON alone would be insufficient.

After journal coverage, the best basis for file selection is the experience of the searcher. A generalist searcher is usually at a disadvantage in searching a specific subject. An information specialist with a good background in a field such as polymer chemistry is well qualified to select the best files to search for his subject area.

TABLE 2.4 Mechanical File—Journal Coverage of Papers Relevant to a Query in the Field of Process Metallurgy

Journal CODEN	No. of references per mechanical file		
	METADEX	CACON	COMPENDEX
AREIAT	2	1	2
BHMMA	—	—	1
CMRJAG	—	—	1
HUTLA7	—	—	1
ISIPBU	5	1	—
JOMTAA	—	1	—
JSMGAX	—	—	1
MTGTBF	—	—	1
MTLUA8	—	—	1
MTTABN	—	—	1
PIHUAC	—	1	—
REMEAH	2	—	—
SJMLAG	—	—	1
STEIA3	1	—	—
SUSRA5	2	—	2
TISJBB	1	3	2
XADRCH	—	1	—
ZEMTAE	—	—	1
Totals	13	8	15

Even the most expert specialist, however, may be thrown off by a search request involving two or more subject areas, for example, "what is the effect of new technology in the plastics field on the world market?" This question requires knowledge of what the new plastics technology is and what markets it might affect—Paper? Containers? Construction? Perhaps our polymer expert, even after clearing up these two problems, is not familiar with the available business or market files. Consultation with an expert in business information may be most helpful. Comparisons of the listings of files for different subject areas may be useful. Here also, SDC's new postings file listing may be of value.

A special limited subject search may require patent searching. Several articles about the unique requirements of patent searching appear in [13–20].

What It is Necessary to Know About a Machine Searchable File

Before a file is searched, the searcher should have some knowledge of the following:

1. Coverage. As discussed above, subject coverage or journal coverage should be investigated. Usually the file producers prepare a reference list of the periodicals covered. The journal list is available in hard copy or in computer searchable tape. If the latter is online, it is usually more frequently updated than the hard copy.

2. The time span of the file—how far back does it go and how often is it updated?

3. Where can one go to get help with unexpected intricacies of the file, or to obtain instructions on optimum searching methods based on indexing policies? In other words, who is the tape producer? The first organization to consult is not the originator of the file but rather the organization that prepares the searchable tape. COMPENDEX is a product of Engineering Index, Inc. but the tape that is searched online is prepared by Lockheed or SDC.

4. Searchable and printable data base elements present on the tape. In general, anything that can be searched can be printed and vice versa, although of course this is dependent upon the search and print programs that can be set up by the tape processor. For instance, it could be possible to search on selected major and minor index terms, but not to print them out. Some programs are limited in just this way, but they are undesirable from the searcher's point of view because it is not possible to tell what index terms caused the hits. Table 2.5 shows the difference between the printable (and searchable) surrogates for the COMPENDEX file as prepared by Lockheed and SDC.

5. The search program form—what codes must be keyed into the computer to perform the searching manipulations desired.

6. User aids such as vocabulary index lists, thesauri, manuals detailing coding procedures required for searching, and journals and conferences covered.

7. Special procedures for obtaining the accessioned documents. For instance, for COMPENDEX, document loan services are available from the library of the Engineering Society, as are document delivery and reprographic services.

TABLE 2.5 Comparison of Searchable and Printable Surrogates of COMPENDEX File for SDC and Lockheed as of 1978

	Lockheed		SDC	
Surrogate	Searchable	Printed	Searchable	Printed
E. I. no.	—	X	X	X
Processor's no.	X	X	—	—
Title	X	X	X	X
Author	X	X	X	X
Author affiliation	X	X	X	X
Major heading	X	X	X	X
Minor heading	X	X	X	X
Identifiers	X	X	X	X
Card alert no.	X	X	X	X
Bibliographic source	—	X	—	X
Abstract	X	X	—	X
CODEN	X	X	X	X
Category codes	—	—	X	X

Sources: Data compiled with permission from Lockheed Missiles & Space Company, Inc. and System Development Corporation.

8. If the user is obtaining tapes and processing by his own program, rather than by searching online or using a retrieval service, then he must know the tape specifications, such as the code (BCD, EBCDIC), density, number of tracks, presence and kind of labels, and the record format (blocked or unblocked), number of bytes per block, number of bits per byte.

If an organization going into the information retrieval business is preparing or acquiring its own tapes for searching, it should be staffed with information scientists with background and experience in performing searches in the subject area of interest. If the organization decides to make use of online services such as those of Lockheed, SDC, or BRS, then library or professional personnel should be trained in the workshops offered by commercial services and academic training centers.

GOVERNMENT FILES

The information files available for automated searching are from three different kinds of sources: government agencies, professional societies or university-sponsored organizations, and commercial organizations whose business is the gathering and selling of information in a wide or narrow subject field.

Examples of files produced by government agencies are NTIS (from the National Technical Information Service), NASA (from the National Aeronautics and Space Administration), MEDLARS and MEDLINE (from the National Library of Medicine), ENVIRON (from the Environmental Protection Agency) and EEDB (from the Energy Research and Development Administration). Table 2.6 lists the organizations supplying online searches of the above government files, and the general subject matter coverage of each file. More information about each file can be obtained from [1].

From the "Producer Index" of [1], it is possible to estimate roughly that there are about 40 U.S. government agency files now available, and about 25 from government agencies of other countries. Although the NTIS file is available from the commercial online sources, most other government files are available from restricted sources only. For instance, MEDLINE is available in Pittsburgh to the public through the University of Pittsburgh's Falk Library of Medicine or from KASC. Only recently has it been made available from the commercial online organization BRS. It should be noted that while the NTIS file covers reports from many government agencies it does not contain every government technical publication. So voluminous are government publications that the memory does not as yet exist that could carry every government publication, except perhaps on a weekly basis.

FILES PRODUCED BY SOCIETIES AND ORGANIZATIONS

In the field of science and technology, many of the most useful files are produced by professional organizations, which represent groups of scientists united by interest in a common subject field such as chemistry, physics, metallurgy, geology, life sciences, or number theory. Examples of such files are COMPENDEX, produced by Engineering Index, Inc.; METADEX, produced by the American Society for Metals; BIOSIS Previews, produced by Biosciences Information Service; CACON, produced by the American Chemical Society (Chemical Abstracts Service); APILIT, produced by the American Petroleum Institute; INSPEC, produced by the Institution of Electrical Engineers, London; ERIC, produced by the Educational Resources Information Center; and SSIE, produced by the Smithsonian Science Information Exchange. Table 2.7 lists the online availability of these typical files and the subjects that they cover.

TABLE 2.6 Examples of Government Files

File	Searches available online from:		Subject coverage
NTIS	BRS Lockheed SDC		Multidisciplinary coverage of technical reports generated by U.S. government sponsored research
NASA (STAR/IAA)	NASA ARAC ESA KASC NC/STRC NERAC WESRAC	Data base is searched online by these organizations for the public	Worldwide coverage of technical report literature related to aerospace information
MEDLARS/MEDLINE	BRS		Worldwide coverage of biomedical journal literature
ENVIRON	EPA online by arrangement		Literature related to environmental science
EEDB	ERDA online by arrangement		International literature relevant to the various energy fields

Source: Data with permission from Ref. 1.

ACADEMIC FILES

Organization-produced files also include files prepared by academic departments specifically for their own use, but often made available to the general public. Among these files are Petroleum Abstracts, from the University of Tulsa; GRID, from the University of California; IDIS, from the University of Iowa; NICEM, from the University of Southern California; RIC, from Iowa State University; and CPA, from Johns Hopkins University. Table 2.8 lists the subject areas and where online searches may be obtained for these files.

TABLE 2.7 Organization Files

File	Available online from:	Subject field
COMPENDEX	CISTI ESA Lockheed SDC	Worldwide coverage of significant engineering literature
METADEX	ESA Lockheed RIT	Metallurgy
BIOSIS Previews	BRS CISTI DIMDI Lockheed SUNY/BCN SDC	Life sciences
CACON	BRS ESA Lockheed NOCI SDC	Worldwide coverage chemistry and chemical engineering
APILIT	SDC	Worldwide coverage of petroleum refining and the petrochemical industry
INSPEC	SDC Lockheed	Electronics, electrical engineering, mathematics, mechanical engineering, physics
ERIC (CIJE)	BRS Lockheed SDC	Education and curriculum materials
SSIE	Lockheed SDC	Summary descriptions of research sponsored by government, some by universities, state and local government, industrial and foreign organizations

Source: Data with permission from Ref. 1.

TABLE 2.8 Academic files

File	Available online from:	Subject field
Petroleum abstracts	SDC	Exploration and production of gas and oil
GRID	University of California (the producer)	Geothermal energy
IDIS	None (see producer for batch searches)	Drugs and drug therapy
NICEM	Lockheed	Nonbook educational media
RIC	None	Solid state physics of rare earth metals, toxicity included
CPA	Johns Hopkins University (the producer)	Chemical propulsion, propellants, explosives, pyrotechnics, materials and construction, safety and hazards

Source: Data with permission from Ref. 1.

COMMERCIALLY PRODUCED FILES

Many commercial ventures have been launched with the purpose of assembling automated sources of information and selling the product. The chief of these in the field of science and technology, and one of the most successful, is the Institute for Scientific Information, Inc. Others include the New York Times Information Services, Inc.; Predicasts; and ABI Inform. Table 2.9 lists the files prepared by these organizations, their subject areas, and the online availability of searches. A review of the growth of one of these successful businesses is contained in [21].

The continual emergence of new files, some of which are either offshoots of old files or subject-oriented files which overlap portions of older files, makes the selection of files to search a matter of keeping up with new offerings and observing the results of old searches.

TABLE 2.9 Commercially Produced Files

Producer	File name	Available online from:	Subject
Institute for Scientific Information	ICRS (Index Chemicus Registry System)	Not available	Synthesis and application of organic chemical compounds
	ISR (Index to Scientific Reviews)	Not available	Worldwide review articles in science
	SCI (Science Citation Index)	Lockheed	Worldwide prime journals of science and engineering
	SSCI (Social Sciences Citation Index)	Lockheed	Worldwide prime journals in social science
The New York Times Information Services, Inc.	The Information Bank	New York Times	News and editorial matter from the New York Times and 60 other newspapers and magazines
Predicasts, Inc.	CMA (Chemical Market Abstracts)	Lockheed	Chemical process industries
	Domestic Statistics	Lockheed	Forecasts, history, and general economics of all industries
	EMA (Equipment Market Abstracts)	Lockheed	Electronics market
	F&S Index	Lockheed	Business, economics, management
	Federal Index	Lockheed	Legislation, hearings, regulations related to business, economics, or management
	International Statistics	Lockheed	Forecasts for industries not in the U.S.A.
	Source Directory	Lockheed	Business, economics, management
ABI Inform	Inform	BRS, SDC Lockheed	Worldwide management and administration

Source: Data with permission from Ref. 1.

Appendix

SUMMARY

In 1976, 52 million records, each an individual bibliographic reference, were available for automated searching. The information explosion has resulted in a growth rate of over 10 million records per year. Over 300 machine searchable files cover a wide range of subject areas in science, technology, education, and commerce. In order to search an automated file it is necessary to know the subject coverage, time span, and format of the file, the searching procedures, and where to get help. Files are prepared by government sources, societies, nonprofit organizations, universities, and commercial producers.

APPENDIX Some Files Available for Subjects in Science and Technology

File	Producer	Number of records as of 1976	Anticipated growth rate per year
ABI Inform	ABI-Inform (Data Courier Inc.)	40,000	14,500
APILIT	American Petroleum Institute	180,000	18,000
BIOSIS Previews	Biosciences Information Service	1,600,000	240,000
CACON	Chemical Abstracts Service	2,333,000	387,000
CMA	Predicasts, Inc.	42,000	14,000
COMPENDEX	Engineering Index, Inc.	496,300	85,000
CPA	Johns Hopkins University	7,200	1,200
Domestic Statistics	Predicasts, Inc.	77,000	20,000
EEDB	Energy Research and Development Administration	165,000	135,000
EMA	Predicasts, Inc.	40,000	12,000
ENVIRON	Environmental Protection Agency	terminated 1974	

APPENDIX (Continued)

File	Producer	Number of records as of 1976	Anticipated growth rate per year
ERIC (RIE/CIJE)	Educational Resources Information Center	222,000	34,500
F & S Index	Predicasts, Inc.	500,000	200,000
Federal Index	Predicasts, Inc.	4,500	50,000
GRID	University of California	2,500	200
ICRS	Institute for Scientific Information	155,000	15,000
IDIS	University of Iowa	55,000	9,000
The Information Bank	The New York Times Information Services, Inc.	over 1,000,000	250,000
INSPEC	Institution of Electrical Engineers	900,000	100,000
International Statistics	Predicasts, Inc.	103,500	20,000
ISMEC	Institution of Electrical Engineers	30,000	15,000
ISR	Institute for Scientific Information	16,000	16,000
MEDLINE	National Library of Medicine	2,000,000	220,000
METADEX	American Society for Metals	300,000	30,000
NASA (STAR/IAA)	U.S. National Aeronautics and Space Administration	776,000	59,000
NICEM	University of Southern California	500,000	45,000
NTIS	National Technical Information Service	360,000	60,000
Petroleum Abstracts	University of Tulsa	165,000	16,000
RIC	Iowa State University	—	—

References

APPENDIX (Continued)

File	Producer	Number of records as of 1976	Anticipated growth rate per year
SCI	Institute for Scientific Information	4,313,335	400,000
Source Directory	Predicasts, Inc.	5,000	—
SSCI	Institute for Scientific Information	95,000	30,000
SSIE	Smithsonian Science Information Exchange, Inc.	200,000	125,000
WAA	American Society for Metals	40,000	6,000

Source: Data with permission from Ref. 1.

REFERENCES

1. Martha E. Williams and Sandra H. Rouse. Computer Readable Bibliographic Data Bases. A Directory and Sourcebook. American Society for Information Science, 1976. A more recent edition is available as this book goes to press, which the reader should be aware of: Martha E. Williams (Ed.). Computer-Readable Data Bases: A Directory and Data Sourcebook, 1979 edition. ASIS publication from Knowledge Industry Publications, Inc., White Plains, New York.
2. U.S. Library of Congress. Science and Technology Division. "Directories Containing Descriptive Information on Nonbibliographic Data Bases. A Selected Bibliography." PB 232 630/4GA. December 1973.
3. James L. Wood, Carolyn Flanagan, and H. E. Kennedy. "Overlap in the Lists of Journals Monitored by BIOSIS, CAS, and EI." JASIS, 23 (1), January-February 1972, p. 36.
4. Charles Oppenheim and Elspeth A. Sutherland. "Studies on Metallurgical Patent Literature. I. The Coverage of Patents by Abstract Journals in Metallurgy." J. Chem. Inf. Comput. Sci., 18(3), 1978, p. 122.
5. Lockheed Missiles and Space Co., Inc. Subject Guide to Dialog Databases. Palo Alto, CA, October 1978.

6. Henry H. Teitelbaum and Donald T. Hawkins. "Database Subject Index." Online 2(2), April 1978, p. 16.
7. Edward M. Arnett and Allen Kent (Eds.). Computer Based Chemical Information. Dekker, New York, 1973.
8. Bart E. Holm, Mary Gertrude Howell, H. Edward Kennedy, Joseph H. Kuney, and James E. Rush. "The status of Chemical Information." J. Chem. Doc., 13(4), November 1973, p. 171.
9. Marjorie R. Hyslop. A Brief Guide to Sources of Metals Information. Information Resources Press, Washington, D. C., 1973.
10. Henry M. Woodburn. Using the Chemical Literature. A Practical Guide. Dekker, New York 1974.
11. Geoffrey Sharp. "Online Business Information." Online, 2(1), January 1978, p. 33.
12. Graeme Hirst. "Discipline Impact Factors: A Method for Determining Core Journal Lists." JASIS 29(4), July 1978, p. 171.
13. Patrick T. O'Leary. "Patent Information Activity of the Technical Information Retrieval Committee of the Manufacturing Chemists' Association." J. Chem. Inf. Comput. Sci. 18(2), May 1978, p. 63.
14. Harry M. Allcock and John W. Lotz. "Patent Intelligence and Technology—Gleaning Pseudopropriatory Information from Publicly Available Data." J. Chem. Inf. Comput. Sci. 18(2), May 1978, p. 65.
15. Wolfgang Pilch and Werner Wratschko. "INPADOC: A Computerized Patent Documentation System." J. Chem. Inf. Comput. Sci. 18(2), May 1978, p. 69.
16. Martin J. Marcus. "Patents and Information." J. Chem. Inf. Comput. Sci. 18(2), May 1978, p. 76.
17. Trisha M. Johns and Dorothy I. Ryno. "Patent Searching in a Pharmaceutical Company." J. Chem. Inf. Comput. Sci. 18(2), May 1978, p. 79.
18. Walker H. Bowman. "Importance of Patents and Information Services to Research Workers." J. Chem. Inf. Comput. Sci. 18(2), May 1978, p. 81.
19. Pauline Newman and Erick I. Hoegberg. "What the Patent Attorney Needs from a Patent Information Point of View." J. Chem. Inf. Comput. Sci. 18(2), May 1978, p. 83.
20. Aldona K. Valicenti. "The Information Chemist's View of the Patent Information Needs of Research Workers and Patent Attorneys." J. Chem. Inf. Comput. Sci. 18(2), May 1978, p. 85.
21. William J. Broad. "Librarian Turned Entrepreneur Makes Millions Off Mere Footnotes." Science 202, November 24, 1978, p. 853.

chapter 3

The Strategy of Mechanized Search

INTRODUCTION

A mechanical search requests, in suitable format, that the computer sort through the information in a file for relevant items. The computer is given key, or entry, terms or codes to be matched with the term or code surrogates of the file items. Those items for which the required match is found are printed out. Figure 3.1 is an example of an item from the National Technical Information Service (NTIS) file. Any of the alphabetic or numeric terms, or surrogates, appearing in Fig. 3.1 could serve as a key, entry, or access point for selecting the item, provided the search program is capable of searching for the given surrogate.

A good search plan, or strategy, must be based on both the characteristics of the search file and the capabilities of the search program. The file characteristics include the format in which a term is presented. For example, will the author's first name appear, or only the first initial? Program capabilities include the coding methods used to identify surrogates. For example, is it possible to use a piece of a word to locate all words built on the same stem? That is, is it possible, for example, to "truncate" after the author's first initial to pick up both first name and initial? File characteristics and program capabilities are discussed in Chap. 6.

Appendix I (page 63) is a flow diagram for the sequence of events that make up a mechanical search for technical literature references, using three separate files.

ENTRY POINTS

Subject Words or Terms

A search may be made using a subject word or term of the sort occurring in titles, index terms, or abstracts. Sometimes a program requires the coding of the term before entry, but almost all searching programs now

COLLECTIVE BARGAINING IN THE BASIC STEEL INDUSTRY: A STUDY OF THE
PUBLIC INTEREST AND THE ROLE OF GOVERNMENT

Department of Labor, Washington, D.C.   (109 200)
 5982E2   FLD:5T   USGRDR6911
Jan 61   312p

ABSTRACT: The report contains an examination of the frequency and intensity of postwar steel strikes compared with those in other industries and a limited analysis of the effect of steel strikes on the economy. A second phase explores such matters as the development of the industry's labor policy, the organization and structure of the Steelworkers, strike techniques, bargaining structures, contract administration, and the area of conflict and accommodation. The economic results of collective bargaining are reviewed. The role of government in steel labor disputes is discussed.

DESCRIPTORS; (*Labor, *Steel industry), (Bargaining, Reviews), Public relations, United States Government, Economics, Interactions, Impact, Wages, Costs, Industrial relations, Labor unions, Management planning

IDENTIFIERS: Strikes, Prices, Inflation(Economics)

Figure 3.1 A searchable item from the NTIS file. (Courtesy U.S. Department of Commerce.)

accept keyboarded alphanumerics. An example of a searchable subject word for the item in Fig. 3.1 is the double-word term COLLECTIVE BARGAINING, which could be submitted to the computer with the instruction "List all items in the file for which the term COLLECTIVE BARGAINING appears." If the search program is only capable of selecting on the basis of "descriptors" or "identifiers," the item in Fig. 3.1 would not be retrieved, since COLLECTIVE BARGAINING does not appear as either a descriptor or an identifier. A search program selection capability by subject can be based on index headings and subheadings, on coordinated index structure, on acceptable index terms, on words in the title, or on "free text"—that is, on any word appearing in the complete item record. The item in Fig. 3.1 would be retrieved by the term COLLECTIVE BARGAINING if the search program selects on the basis of "free-text" or "title" terms.

Various studies [1] have shown that the most effective searches are made on "title plus text" terms. The text is all the alphanumeric material on the tape aside from the title. It may consist of keywords, index terms, notations of content, or abstracts. While titles have been found to be powerful tools for identifying documents, titles may be misleading. If a mechanical search were based on title alone, the item in Fig. 3.2 might be listed from a search for "mechanics of preparing fish for the market," and might not be listed from a search for "the application of non-linear continuum mechanics to studies of elasticity and viscoelasticity." Since the advent of mechanical searching such catchy, metaphoric but nonspecific titles occur less and less frequently.

```
N70-15864      Lehigh Univ.,Bethlehem, Pa. Center for
the Application of Mathematics.
RED HERRING AND SUNDRY UNIDENTIFIED FISH IN NON-LINEAR
CONTINUUM MECHANICS
R. S. Rivlin  Sep. 1969  37 p refs
(Contract N00014-67-A-o370)
(AD-695773: CAM-100-9)  Avail: CFSTI CSCL 20/11
     Since the Second World War, there has been a
rapid development in the non-linear continuum mechanical
theories of elasticity and viscoelasticity. The salient
stages in the development of these theories are discussed.
Various concepts which have been proposed are discussed
critically both with respect to logical status and physi-
cal relevance. These include the principle of material
frame-indifference, certain thermodynamic theories as
they apply to continua, and the axiomatization of
mechanics.                                          TAB
```

Figure 3.2 Example of "red herring" title. (Reproduced from the STAR file of NASA, courtesy National Aeronautics and Space Administration.)

<u>Heading-Subheading Entries</u> The heading-subheading entry is a method used in the card indexes of many libraries. Usually the depth of indexing is not great, each item carrying not more than three or four index terms. A heading-subheading system can be utilized successfully for small, specialized, mechanical files. Frequently such files have grown from the card index of a specialized user. If the indexers and the searchers are the same individuals, such a file is quite capable of producing useful listings.

For instance, the item in Fig. 3.1 might be contained in a file about United States industry, under the heading Steel Industry, subheading Unions. A request for information about unions in the steel industry would result in a printout of all items listed under heading Steel Industry, subheading Unions, and would include the item in Fig. 3.1. A small, specialized, mechanical file of this kind can be prepared to produce the documents themselves in the form of microfiche. This sharply tailored approach is useful for the internal systems of companies, where the kind of information that will be needed is easy to predict.

A large system that makes use of the heading-subheading index approach is the Chemical Abstract Service's CA Subject Index Alert (CASIA) [2]. This is the highly structured Chemical Substance Index and General Subject Index of the CA Volume Indexes, in mechanical form. These indexes consist of headings below which index phrases (notations of content) are entered in alphabetic order, as shown in Fig. 3.3. The indexes are prepared by highly trained subject specialist indexers. In hard copy they yield excellent results. Mechanically, they are usually searched in the free-text (see the section Free Text below), rather than the heading-subheading, mode.

The Strategy of Mechanized Search

761GS — JULY-DEC 1976 GENERAL SUBJECT INDEX — Fibrinogens

low-loss light-focusing, 102195q
networks, in communications, location of fiber faults in, 85484p
optical absorption of, gamma ray effect on, 95285r
phosphosilicate glass-based, 102194p
polymers for, R 12550x
polystyrene for, light transmittance of, effect of mol. wt. and residual monomer content on, 109093p
quartz glass tube lining for, with silica, P 96289y
radiation probes for sodium iodide, for plutonium detection in tracheobronchial lymph nodes, 11458m
radiation response of, 11765g
Raman spectra in studies of, 133491n
refractometer employing, for use in liq. chromatog., 151663z
silica glass for fibers for, boron oxide and titanium oxide in doping of, 50826z
sodium borosilicate, for optical communication, 102196r
sodium borosilicate glass for, contg. copper and iron and antimony oxide in core, P 165562c
spectral loss of low-hydroxyl-content, 114553t
in telecommunications, R 135048x
titanium oxide-doped vitreous silica fibers for, app. for continuous manuf. of, P 98370y
transmission in, R 169954t
transmission line sources, high radiance light emitting diodes on, 70572s
transmission research on, R 132896m
vitreous silica
  doping of, 129271y, P 165571e
  germanium oxide-doped, P 145071z
  titanium oxide-doped, P 145071z
vitreous silica and silicate glass for, copper and iron detn. in, 181342m
vitreous silica doped with titanium oxide for, P 36655m
vitreous silica doping with germanium oxide for, germanium oxide loss prevention in, P 82412c
vitreous silica fibers with boron silicate glass inner layer, P 98350s
vitreous silica tube coating with aluminum oxide for, P 112055h
waveguides, absorption induced in, by electron-gamma-ray irradn., 88006j
waveguides for,   optical, 151654x
wave splitting coupler, made with carbon dioxide laser, 134021w
zero gravity-grown, 134027c

Fibers
acrylic acid-styrene copolyer contg., for wall materials, P 6954r
anal. of, forensic, R 117455y
animal, prodn. and properties of, R 22634s
assocd. with ceramics, as thermal insulators in high temp. reactors, 197030q
casein-gluten, spinning of, 141569j
cellulose, pyrolysis of, structure in relation to, 14454lte

removal of, from pulping effluents, R 181820r
sodium chloride-sodium fluoride eutectic, zero-gravity growth of, 134027c
spinning of, waste water from, treatment of, by foam flotation, 166137e
stabilizers for, aroyldibenzofurans as UV, P 94166p
structural characteristics of, 144512w
structure of repeatedly deformed, dynamic mech. properties in relation to, 64583e
styrene grafted cellulosic, phys. and mech. properties of, 125596k
in surface-wave delay lines, R 55093t
swelling of carboxyl-contg., 64578g
waste
  asphalt contg., for thermal insulators, P 64961b
  fleece from, impregnation with bitumens for brickwork insulation and roof coverings, P 197134f
waterproofing of, by grafting with siloxanes by irradn., P 95765v

Fibril
formation of, in polyamide-polystyrene plastics, maleic anhydride-styrene copolymer for prevention of, P 109346y
of low-d. polyethylene, formation of, in uniaxial stretching, 47235a
of polymers, structure of, small-angle x-ray scattering in relation to, 78557m

Fibrinogens (*blood-coagulation factors I*)
abnormal, peptide map and sialic acids in variants of Zurich II, 190228f
absorption of, on glass and polyethylene, extracorporeal circulation in relation to, 166617m
Aα-chain, degrdn. products of, antigenic determinants of, 61293z
in adaptation, to high altitude, 3274h
adrenaline-heparin complex, anticoagulation system response to factor XIII and, 118824f
adsorption of
  by biomaterials, 149085u
  at electrode surfaces, ir spectrometry of, 173726z
  to polyethylene, erythrocytes effect on, 166599z
  on polyvinyl chloride, phthalate plasticizer effect on, 10397d
  to polyvinyl chloride), 166598f
  amino acid sequence of C-terminal region of, 118236q
Anthio effect on level of, 104918b
antibodies to, iodine-131-labeled, for scintigraphy in inflammation, 1845w
antigenic determinants of peptides of, 3711y
antigens and disulfides of, R 3646f
bacterial binding to polystyrene inhibition by, 139666v
of blood
  in atherosclerosis, mineral waters bathing effect on, 91713d
  in desiminated intravascular coagulation, amidinophenylpyruvate effect on, 186730w
  fetus growth retardation in relation to, 61047x

Fibrinogens

Consult Vol. 76-85 Cumulative Index Guide Before Using This Index

deficiency of, exptl., 18643b
degrdn. of, streptokinase effect on, 18036f
degrdn. products
  detn. of, technical guide for, 106343j
  heart response to, 13730t
  in lung embolism, 140893y
  phagocytosis and reticuloendothelial catabolism response to, coagulation disorder in relation to, 141224t
  sepn. and properties of, 172970n
degrdn. products and, detn. of, staining reagent for, P 185774n
degrdn. products of,
  biol. properties of, 91234y
  of blood plasma in puerperium, 75753m
  blood platelet aggregation and bleeding response to hypofibrinogenemia and, 3580e
  of blood serum and urine, in kidney disease, R 1-3014q
  of blood serum and urine in exercise, 3337f
  of blood serum in pulmonary embolism, 18620s
  characterization of, of blood serum, 139338q
  chromatog. and electrophoresis of, R 1236y
  in coronary artery disease, 140843g
  detn. in blood serum of, immunol., 2101n
  detn. in blood serum of newborns, microbiol., 88096g
  detn. in urine, 173792t
  detn. of, by hemagglutination inhibition immunoassay, 106330c
  detn. of, by immunoassay, 61195u
  detn. of, pulmonary embolism in relation to, 2144d
  detn. of, in urine, P 106393a
  fragment E in relation to, 16741h
  immunol. reaction with antiserum to fibrinopeptide A, 74523z
  renal catabolism and uremia in clearance of, 3135e
  thrombin in relation to, R 44067m
  derivs., in prothrombin activation, 31082n
  detection of, in liver, immunoenzymic, fixation in relation to, 106317d
detn. of
  by automated nephelometry, of blood, 106187n
  in blood plasma, sulfite and thrombin methods for, 119300p
  in blood plasma by electroimmunodiffusion, 69722b
  degrdn. products inhibition of, 106376x
  plasma stabilized prepn. as std. for, P 106396d
Detroit, activity and structure of, 121080q
dextran-erythrocyte membrane interaction in relation to, 15822y
D fragment, neoantigenic determinants of, detn. by

cellulose derivs., as tablet disintegrant, P 25393y
cellulosic
  adsorbed liqs. on, nuclear magnetic relaxation of, 34509t
  formation of, by bacteria, 29748r
  helical super structure of, detn. of, by light scattering anal., 22645w
  kraft bleached, beating effect on structure of, 34883k
collagen
  calcium detn. in prodn. of, by flame spectrophotometry, 64810b
  prepn. of, from leather industry wastes, 64806g
  composites from aluminum and plastics reinforced with, bending behavior of laminated, 111724p
  composites reinforced by, R 143857a
  crystal structure models from balls of, 71047m
  detn. of, in Egyptian rice, 7571a
  diffusion and sorption of dyes in, B 64638b
  electrosurface properties of, in dispersions with dyes, electrolyte effect on, 144560k
  embedding compn. for microscopic observation of cross section of, beeswax-paraffin-pigment mixts. as, P 22692j
  endurance of, mechanism of, R 178600d
  filters for, P 96214b
  finishing and processing agents for, R 144501s
  formation of, B 178867f
  graft polymn. on, R 109872a
  hard elastic, morphol. of, R 63718r
  hemp, mercerization of, crystallinity, crystallite size and orientation in relation to, 109907g
  high-temp. resistant, high modulus, R 95581g
  hollow
    as dialyzers for artificial kidney, R 25295t
    in enzyme reactors, simulation model of, 44900c
    hydroxy group-contg., modifiers for, fibroin hydrolyzates as, 34468d
    identification of, in forensic science, by gas chromatog., 154653g
    interfacial potential of, dyeing properties in relation to, R 178802f
  laminated plastics reinforced by, interlaminar stress in, anal. of, 193724a
  laser application to, 109903c
  metal composites reinforced with, R 14737s
  plastic laminates reinforced by, vibrational mixing of, 34167e
  polyesters reinforced by, with reduced filler sepn. and molding shrinkage, P 161262g
  protein
    crosslinking of, by peroxides or γ-irradn. in dyeing, 34517u
    spinning of, 19362w, P 19108Zr
    structural stability of, in sodium bicarbonate solns., 122110m
    surfactant treatment of, for improved dyeability, P 7202f
  qual. and quant. anal. of, R 125557y

in hyperlipoproteinemia, blood coagulation in relation to, 121130f
of newborns, maturity effect on, 193366z
phenformin effect on, in hypercholesterolemia, 40747k
in pregnancy with fetal growth retardation, 76024m
after pulmonary circulation, ether effect on, 28724t
trauma effect on, sympatholytic in relation to, 56953k
in blood coagulation, R 157403m
of blood plasma
  in autotransfusion, citrate and heparin effect on, 60572c
  in cholestasis, 121151p
  dextran depletion of, in carcinosarcoma, 138043c
  dextran sulfate effect on, in diabetes and arteriosclerosis, 87518b
  endotoxin and turpentine effect on, granulocyte in relation to, 117542z
  ethylestrenol and phenformin effect on, in heart ischemia model, 104040j
  furazabol decrease of, 72687g
  hyperlipoproteinemia and arteriosclerosis in relation to, 3579m
  in metabolic disorders, 44575a
  in methylguanidine intoxication, uremia in relation to, 31332u
  in myocardial infarction, 107206d
  in neoplasia, 18661f
  spleen in relation to, 140483q
  structure and metab. of, cobalt effect on, 134549c
vasodilators effect on, 40911j
of blood platelet, 18001r
blood platelet adhesion enhancement by, 107004m
blood platelet and inert particle aggregation induction by thrombin in response to, 91235z
of blood platelets, in development, 44252t

radioimmunoassay, 89668z
in diseases, blood viscosity in relation to, 61134v
disulfide group in N-terminal region of, structure in relation to, 29747q
evolution of, R 118015s
exercise effect on, 60785z, 60786a, 60787b
fibrin gel elastic modulus in relation to, 30326h
fibrin monomer complex formation from, estrogen effect on, 153373e
fibronectin crosslinking by activated blood-coagulation factor XIII in response to, 169914v
fluorescence quenching of, by salts, 15641p
formation and hydrolysis of, thermodns. of, 60565c
formation of
  15800q
  by hepatoma, 121410x
  by liver in arthritis, 107132b
  by liver in inflammation, 18368r
glass surfaces coated with, blood platelet adhesion to, red cells effect on, 51715z
glycopeptide of β chain of, amino acid sequence of peptide moiety of, 188057f
of hemocyte, of crayfish, 106825t
in hemodialysis, 31359h
of hemolymph, of crayfish in ecdysis, 30871g
heparin complexes, formation of, mechanism of, 157953k
hepatitis B surface antigen in com. prepns. of, 83148t
of horseshoe crab, gelation of, by endotoxin-= activated clotting enzyme, 173018v
hydrolysis of, by alveolar macrophage and leukocyte, 30726d
hydrolysis product, blood-coagulation factor V as, 140467u
in hyperbaric hypoxia, 175228n
hypothalamus emotiogenic zones stimulation effect on, of blood, 91321z
iodine-131 labeled, scintigraphy with, of thrombus, 1845x
iodopeptide interaction with, anticoagulant activity in relation to, 56594u
labeling of
  by iodine-125, lactoperoxidase in, 16673n
  by technetium-99 metastable, P 89787n
in lung alveolar tissue, 90936s
maleylated deriv., in blood coagulation, 44316s
metab. and pathophysiol. of, R 140720q
metab. of
  75663d
  fibrinolysis inhibition effect on, 18006w
  in liver during perfusion, streptokinase effect on, 44373h
  in thrombosis, R 44507e
  metabolic disorders of, R 18331y
  mol. mass change in, in disseminated intravascular coagulation and thrombosis, 61062y
Paris I, hydrolysis of, by plasmin, 157217d

Figure 3.3 Partial page from Chemical Abstracts General Subject Index, July-December 1976. (Material reprinted from Chemical Abstracts Service publications and services is copyrighted by the American Chemical Society and is reproduced with permission. No further copying is permitted.)

Coordinated Indexes   An extension of the simple heading-subheading method of search is the "coordinated index" method. An example of a coordinated index is the Medical Subject Headings (MESH) [3], which by means of a tree structure such as shown in Fig. 3.4 displays for a given term related indexing headings used by the indexer for the documents in the MEDLINE-MEDLARS file, and therefore alerts the user to the useful words in the file. For instance, in Fig. 3.4, for the term DRUG DEPENDENCE, related terms DRUG ADDICTION, DRUG HABITUATION, NARCOTICS, and SOCIAL PROBLEMS are shown. By using MESH tree structures at the cited number, entries related to the subject are also found: DRUG WITHDRAWAL SYMPTOMS, GLUE SNIFFING, MORPHINE ADDICTION, and HEROIN ADDICTION. A section containing the categorized, hierarchic structures is contained within the yearly issues of MESH and should be consulted when one is preparing to search the MEDLARS data base.

Lists of Acceptable Index Terms   Many file processors provide the indexer and user with a "thesaurus" which lists acceptable terms. A sample page from the NASA Thesaurus [4] is shown in Fig. 3.5. Such thesauri are, in general, not as well structured as the MESH. In addition, because of the great numbers of possible synonymous terms and the inconsistencies in the preparation of cross references, the thesauri usually require that the searcher use his imagination to outguess the indexer. Nevertheless, without the help of such thesauri the task would be more difficult. The thesaurus or dictionary for a file may also list total postings to each term. The postings are useful in determining whether a term used in a search should be modified by requesting the presence of another term or terms. Figure 3.6 shows a sample from such a postings dictionary. The term AUTOMOTIVE is linked with 848 abstracts in the COMPENDEX file. Another term should be required to limit the output. A rather extensive set of postings dictionaries is now published by Lockheed under the name DIALIST, and is available in microfiche [5]. An example of a listing is shown in Fig. 3.6. As of Summer 1977, DIALIST includes the following postings dictionaries:

1. Engineering and Technology. Contains NTIS/GRA; EI/COMPENDEX; INSPEC/Electrical and Electronic, and Computer and Control Abstracts; INSPEC/ISMEC-Mechanical Engineering.
2. Sciences I. Contains CAS/CA Condensates; BA/BIOSIS Previews; ISI/SCISEARCH; INSPEC/Physics.
3. Sciences II. Contains CAS/CA Condensates; BA/BIOSIS Previews; ISI/SCISEARCH; NAL/CAIN (AGRICOLA).
4. Social Sciences. Contains NIE/ERIC (Full text); APA/Psychological Abstracts; ISI/Social SCISEARCH; CEC/Exceptional Children Abstracts (Full text).

Free Text   The fourth way in which subject words or terms may be accessed is by the free-text method. When a subject term is applied to the file by a program operating in the free-text mode, there are no restrictions

Entry Points

DROWNING
C21.866.304
G3.850.110.500
C23.240.393
see related
 IMMERSION
 RESUSCITATION

DROWSINESS see SLEEP STAGES

DRUG ABUSE
F1.145.332+
I1.880.735.295+
F3.498+
68
see related
 DRUG AND NARCOTIC CONTROL

DRUG ABUSE, SPORTS see DOPING IN SPORTS

DRUG ADDICTION see DRUG DEPENDENCE

DRUG ADMINISTRATION, INTRANASAL see ADMINISTRATION, INTRANASAL

DRUG ADMINISTRATION, ORAL see ADMINISTRATION, ORAL

DRUG ADMINISTRATION SCHEDULE
E5.300.310
75
X   ADMINISTRATION SCHEDULE, DRUG

DRUG ADMINISTRATION, TOPICAL see ADMINISTRATION, TOPICAL

DRUG ADULTERATION see DRUG CONTAMINATION

DRUG A[...]
I1.880.604.[...]
68; NARC[...]
X   NAR[...]
XR DRU[...]
XR LEGI[...]

DRUG A[...]
G12.361.31[...]
68
see related
 NARC[...]

DRUG BENE[...]
 SERVICE[...]

DRUG CATA[...]

DRUG C[...]
D26.394[...]
73

DRUG COM[...]
 COMMIT[...]

DRUG C[...]
E5.916.27[...]
see related
 BIOPHARMACEUTICS

DRUG CONTAINERS AND CLOSURES see DRUG PACKAGING

DRUG CONTAMINATION
G3.850.360
76; DRUG ADULTERATION was heading 1963-76
X   DRUG ADULTERATION

DRUG DEPENDENCE
F3.709.597.285+
76; was see under DRUG ADDICTION 1969-75, was see under DRUG ABUSE 1968; DRUG ADDICTION was heading 1963-75
X   DRUG ADDICTION
X   DRUG HABITUATION
XR NARCOTICS
XR SOCIAL PROBLEMS

DRUG DETOXICATION, METABOLIC see METABOLIC DETOXICATION, DRUG

DRUG ERUPTIONS see DERMATITIS MEDICAMENTOSA

DRUG EVALUATION
E5.337.310
74
G12.330

DRUG HABITUATION see DRUG DEPENDENCE

DRUG HYPERSENSITIVITY
C20.543.206+
66; was DRUG ALLERGY 1963-65

DRUG IMPLANTS
D26.394.225.276.315
75

DRUG INCOMPATIBILITY
E5.916.290
73

DRUG INDUSTRY
J1.576.318+
XR TECHNOLOGY, PHARMACEUTICAL

DRUG INFORMATION SERVICES see under INFORMATION SERVICES

DRUG INSURANCE see INSURANCE, PHARMACEUTICAL SERVICES

DRUG INTERACTIONS
G12.361+
72

DRUG LABELING
E5.780.310
J1.576.318.477
68
X   LABELING, DRUG
E5.916.310
J1.790.310

F3 – BEHAVIORAL AND MENTAL DISORDERS

BEHAVIORAL AND MENTAL DISORDERS (NON MESH)
 MENTAL DISORDERS
  PERSONALITY DISORDERS
   ANTISOCIAL PERSONALITY

ANTISOCIAL PERSONALITY	F3.709.597.55
CYCLOTHYMIC PERSONALITY ·	F3.709.597.202
DRUG DEPENDENCE	F3.709.597.285
DRUG WITHDRAWAL SYMPTOMS	F3.709.597.285.60
GLUE SNIFFING	F3.709.597.285.115
MORPHINE ADDICTION	F3.709.597.285.220
HEROIN ADDICTION	F3.709.597.285.220.85
HYSTERICAL PERSONALITY	F3.709.597.357
OBSESSIVE–COMPULSIVE PERSONALITY ·	F3.709.597.570
PARANOID PERSONALITY DISORDER ·	F3.709.597.625
PASSIVE–AGGRESSIVE PERSONALITY ·	F3.709.597.671
PASSIVE–DEPENDENT PERSONALITY ·	F3.709.597.671.600

F1.145.332.   F3.498.448   I1.880.735.[...]

74

DRUG STABILITY
E5.916.330
68

DRUG STORAGE
E5.916.350
68

DRUG SYNERGISM
G12.361.477
66
see related
 PESTICIDE SYNERGISTS
X   DRUG POTENTIATION

DRUG THERAPY
E2.319+
see related
 MEDICATION ERRORS
X   CHEMOTHERAPY
X   PHARMACOTHERAPY
XR PHARMACOLOGY

+ INDICATES THERE ARE INDENTED DESCRIPTORS IN MESH TREE STRUCTURES AT THIS NUMBER

Figure 3.4   Partial page from MESH (Medical Subject Headings) for 1979, with insert from Numbered MESH Tree Structures in the same volume. (Published by the National Library of Medicine.   Courtesy Public Health Service, National Institutes of Health.)

NITRYL FLUORIDES   **NASA THESAURUS (ALPHABETICAL LISTING)**

```
NITRYL CHLORIDES-(CON'T)
     . . NITRYL CHLORIDES
   NITROGEN COMPOUNDS
   . NITRYL CHLORIDES

NITRYL FLUORIDES
  GS   FLUORINE COMPOUNDS
       . FLUORIDES
       . . NITRYL FLUORIDES
       NITROGEN COMPOUNDS
       . NITRYL FLUORIDES

NOAA SATELLITES
  GS   SATELLITES
       . ARTIFICIAL SATELLITES
       . . METEOROLOGICAL SATELLITES
       . . . NOAA SATELLITES
       . . . . NOAA 2 SATELLITE
       . . . . NOAA 3 SATELLITE
       . EARTH SATELLITES
       . . METEOROLOGICAL SATELLITES
       . . . NOAA SATELLITES
       . . . . NOAA 2 SATELLITE
       . . . . NOAA 3 SATELLITE

NOAA 2 SATELLITE
  GS   SATELLITES
       . ARTIFICIAL SATELLITES
       . . METEOROLOGICAL SATELLITES
       . . . NOAA SATELLITES
       . . . . NOAA 2 SATELLITE
       . EARTH SATELLITES
       . . METEOROLOGICAL SATELLITES
       . . . NOAA SATELLITES
       . . . . NOAA 2 SATELLITE

NOAA 3 SATELLITE
  GS   SATELLITES
       . ARTIFICIAL SATELLITES
       . . METEOROLOGICAL SATELLITES
       . . . NOAA SATELLITES
       . . . . NOAA 3 SATELLITE
       . EARTH SATELLITES
       . . METEOROLOGICAL SATELLITES
       . . . NOAA SATELLITES
       . . . . NOAA 3 SATELLITE

NOBELIUM
  GS   CHEMICAL ELEMENTS
       . ACTINIDE SERIES
       . . TRANSURANIUM ELEMENTS
       . . . NOBELIUM
       . NUCLIDES
       . . ISOTOPES
       . . . RADIOACTIVE ISOTOPES
       . . . . TRANSURANIUM ELEMENTS
       . . . . . NOBELIUM
       HEAVY ELEMENTS
       . TRANSURANIUM ELEMENTS
       . . NOBELIUM
       METALS
       . ACTINIDE SERIES
       . . TRANSURANIUM ELEMENTS
       . . . NOBELIUM

NOBLE GASES
  USE  RARE GASES

NOBLE METALS
  UF   PRECIOUS METALS
  GS   METALS
       . NOBLE METALS
       . . GOLD
       . . . GOLD ISOTOPES
       . . . . GOLD 198
       . . RUTHENIUM
       . . . RUTHENIUM ISOTOPES
       . . SILVER
       . . . SILVER ISOTOPES
  RT   ∞GROUP 1B COMPOUNDS

NOCTILUCENCE
  USE  LUMINESCENCE
```

```
NOCTILUCENT CLOUDS
  GS   CLOUDS
       . CLOUDS (METEOROLOGY)
       . . NOCTILUCENT CLOUDS
  RT   LUMINESCENCE

NOCTURNAL VARIATIONS
  GS   VARIATIONS
       . MAGNETIC VARIATIONS
       . . NOCTURNAL VARIATIONS
       . PERIODIC VARIATIONS
       . . NOCTURNAL VARIATIONS
  RT   DIURNAL VARIATIONS
       GEOMAGNETIC MICROPULSATIONS
       GEOMAGNETIC PULSATIONS

NODES (STANDING WAVES)
  RT   ANTINODES
       HARMONICS
       RESONANT FREQUENCIES
       STANDING WAVES
       VIBRATION
       WAVELENGTHS
       ∞WAVES

NODULES
  RT   LEGUMINOUS PLANTS
       PARTICLES
       SPHERES
       SPHERULITES

∞NOISE
  SN   (USE OF A MORE SPECIFIC TERM
       IS RECOMMENDED--CONSULT THE
       TERMS LISTED BELOW)
  RT   BACKGROUND NOISE
       CONTINUOUS NOISE
       EFFECTIVE PERCEIVED NOISE
       LEVELS
       ELECTROMAGNETIC NOISE
       HUM
       INFORMATION THEORY
       NOISE (SOUND)
       NOISE PROPAGATION
       NOISE SPECTRA
       RANDOM NOISE
       SIGNAL TO NOISE RATIOS
       SPATIAL FILTERING
       WHITE NOISE

NOISE (SOUND)
  UF   NOISE HAZARDS
  GS   ELASTIC WAVES
       . SOUND WAVES
       . . NOISE (SOUND)
       . . . AERODYNAMIC NOISE
       . . . AIRCRAFT NOISE
       . . . . JET AIRCRAFT NOISE
       . . . SONIC BOOMS
       . . . ENGINE NOISE
       . . . . ROCKET ENGINE NOISE
       . . . THERMAL NOISE
  RT   ACOUSTICS
       AEOLIAN TONES
       AIRCRAFT HAZARDS
       AUDITORY STIMULI
       AUDITORY TASKS
       BACKGROUND NOISE
       ECHOES
       EFFECTIVE PERCEIVED NOISE
       LEVELS
       FLIGHT HAZARDS
       HUMAN FACTORS ENGINEERING
       HYPERSONIC SHOCK
       JET BLAST EFFECTS
       LOUDNESS
       MUFFLERS
       NOISE INJURIES
       OPERATIONAL HAZARDS
       RANDOM NOISE
       RANDOM VIBRATION
       REVERBERATION
       SHOCK WAVES
       SOUND PRESSURE
       UNDERWATER ACOUSTICS
       WHITE NOISE
```

```
NOISE ATTENUATION
  USE  NOISE REDUCTION

NOISE ELIMINATION
  USE  NOISE REDUCTION

NOISE GENERATORS
  RT   ELECTROMAGNETIC NOISE
       ∞GENERATORS
       RADIO FREQUENCY
       INTERFERENCE
       RANDOM NOISE
       SOUND GENERATORS
       SOUND PROPAGATION

NOISE HAZARDS
  USE  HAZARDS
       NOISE (SOUND)

NOISE INJURIES
  GS   INJURIES
       . NOISE INJURIES
  RT   EAR PROTECTORS

NOISE INTENSITY
  RT   AIRCRAFT NOISE
       AUDITORY STIMULI
       EFFECTIVE PERCEIVED NOISE
       LEVELS
       ELECTROMAGNETIC NOISE
       ∞INTENSITY
       PSYCHOACOUSTICS
       SIRENS
       SOUND INTENSITY

NOISE MEASUREMENT
  GS   ACOUSTIC MEASUREMENTS
       . NOISE MEASUREMENT
  RT   AERODYNAMIC NOISE
       AIRCRAFT NOISE
       BACKGROUND NOISE
       JET AIRCRAFT NOISE
       LOUDNESS
       ∞MEASUREMENT
       NOISE (SOUND)
       SOUND INTENSITY

NOISE METERS
  SN   (LIMITED TO ACOUSTIC NOISE)
  GS   MEASURING INSTRUMENTS
       . NOISE METERS
  RT   ACOUSTIC MEASUREMENTS
       FIELD INTENSITY METERS
       PRESSURE MEASUREMENTS

NOISE POLLUTION
  GS   POLLUTION
       . NOISE POLLUTION
  RT   ACOUSTICS
       AUDIO FREQUENCIES
       ENVIRONMENT EFFECTS
       ENVIRONMENT POLLUTION
       ENVIRONMENTAL QUALITY
       HUMAN REACTIONS
       HUMAN TOLERANCES
       PHYSIOLOGICAL EFFECTS
       PHYSIOLOGICAL FACTORS
       SOUND WAVES

NOISE PROPAGATION
  RT   ACOUSTICS
       COHERENCE COEFFICIENT
       CONTINUOUS NOISE
       FAR FIELDS
       NOISE SPECTRA
       SIGNAL TO NOISE RATIOS
       SOUND PROPAGATION

NOISE REDUCTION
  UF   NOISE ATTENUATION
       NOISE ELIMINATION
       NOISE SUPPRESSORS
  RT   ACOUSTIC ATTENUATION
       ACOUSTIC DUCTS
       ACOUSTICS
       AERODYNAMIC NOISE
```

Figure 3.5   Partial page from <u>NASA Thesaurus</u>. (Courtesy National Aeronautics and Space Administration.)

Entry Points

INDEX TERM	NTIS GRA	EI COMP	INSPEC EE&C	ISMEC
AUTOMORPHISM GROUP			13	
AUTOMORPHISM GROUPS			5	
AUTOMORPHISMS	55	7	30	
AUTO		11		
AUTOMOTIVE	734	848	509	158
AUTOMOTIVE AERODYNAMIC AND ROLLING R		2		
AUTOMOTIVE APPLICATION		22		
AUTOMOTIVE APPLICATIONS		11	4	8
AUTOMOTIVE COMPONENTS	4		3	4
AUTOMOTIVE CONTROL		2		
AUTOMOTIVE CRASH INJURY RESEARCH	5			
AUTOMOTIVE ELECTRONICS			5	
AUTOMOTIVE EMISSION CONTROL		9		

Figure 3.6 Sample of merged-term index from <u>Dialist Postings Dictionary</u> as published by Lockheed in [5]. Terms from several files have been merged in this list. (Reproduced with permission by Lockheed Missiles & Space Company, Inc.)

upon the selection of the term, since it may be taken from title, descriptors, journal name, author, abstract, affiliate organization, or even the full document, if the latter is in the mechanical file. The term need not be taken from a list of acceptable terms. This method permits the identification of documents by newly coined or newly popular descriptors. In this sense the method is most rewarding, since a newly popular word or phrase is usually incorporated into the title of publications by those who wish to ride the wave. An example of such a newly popular (in the 1970s) subject is recombinant DNA.

Most search programs now carry functions that enable the searcher to specify a string of words in a given order. In the PIRETS [6] program the connector "adjacent," abbreviated to adj, permits the specification that two words such as "stainless" and "steel" be searched for side by side and in that order:

STAINLESS adj STEEL

On the DIALOG [5] program the specification is:

STAINLESS (W) STEEL

The number of words which might intervene between the two words can also be specified:

MARINE (W) CORROSION

will identify "marine corrosion";

MARINE (2W) CORROSION

will identify "marine environment producing corrosion" as well as "marine corrosion."

MARINE (F) CORROSION

will identify "corrosion occurring in a marine environment," when it occurs in a single field such as notation of content, title, or abstract, as well as "marine corrosion" and "marine environment producing corrosion."

For free-text searching, the program may have "stop words," words not included in coding the material into the file. Examples of such words are "of," "the," and "for." The search program may not necessarily "stop" the same words when they are used in the search strategy. It is wise to know how the program works. The descriptor TURN OF THE CENTURY could appear in the coded file in that form, for which the search strategy should be TURN next to OF next to THE next to CENTURY. If, however, "of" and "the" are stop words, they are not included in the coded text and the phrase could be identified only by TURN next to CENTURY. There can also be differences within the file in the coding of index terms as opposed to textual material such as titles, notations of content, and abstracts. For example, an index term could be MANAGEMENT OF INFORMATION and matching during search would occur only if the full alphabetic string including OF was present in the search term. If the search program operated in free text, however, MANAGEMENT OF INFORMATION could occur in the textual material coded as MANAGEMENT next to INFORMATION, and the search strategy should request MANAGEMENT next to INFORMATION. In order to also pick up on the index term MANAGEMENT OF INFORMATION, the strategy should request MANAGEMENT with one or less words intervening before INFORMATION.

Care must be exercised when the free text mode is used to search entire items. For example, if the term BROWN is used to mean the color, then searching must be restricted to title and keyword fields; if the term is searched on the author field, it may lead to a hit on the author "Brown." Sometimes the occurrence of a technical word such as "polymer" in a journal title can give a worthwhile hit when linked to another term, but more often technical terms occurring in journal titles may confuse the results. For example, the periodical "New York Times" when coupled with the title "Energy Blackouts in Japan," would result in a nonrelevant hit in answer to an inquiry about blackouts in New York. Many programs are now set to search in free-text mode the title, keywords, and abstract if present, rather than the whole item, while retaining the option of searching author, journal, or source by identifying the fields to be searched.

While subject searching is the most frequent approach to obtaining information from mechanical files, the nonsubject-derived surrogates such as author, corporate source, or journal may offer an efficient method to obtain certain kinds of information [7, 8].

Author Names

One of the most definitive surrogates for a particular document is the name of the author, usually with the approximate time of publication, and the subject area. There are many ways to enter an author's name in a file as shown below:

    HEDGEHOPPER, JOHN CALHOUN
    HEDGEHOPPER, J. C.
    HEDGEHOPPER, JOHN C.
    JOHN CALHOUN HEDGEHOPPER
    J. C. HEDGEHOPPER
    JOHN C. HEDGEHOPPER

It is necessary to know the format in which the author name is coded in the file. Even when many files are made available by one commercial source, it should not be assumed that the author names are coded in the same way for every file, because file processors in general code the files into the data bank as they are presented to them by the file suppliers. Efforts are being made to standardize bibliographic references [9], but unless considerable money is spent, the back files will undoubtedly remain as they are now.

It is necessary for searching to know whether the surname appears followed by a comma, by a semicolon, or by a blank and then two initials, or whether the first name and initial appear first followed by surname. The most common form is

    HEDGEHOPPER, J. C.

The recommended way of searching is:

    HEDGEHOPPER, J

with a truncation sign meaning any occurrence of the name HEDGEHOPPER followed by a J, regardless of what comes after the J. Such an entry will not pick up a misspelling of the name, for instance the entry

    HEGDEHOPPER, J.

Sometimes, and this is true also of misspelled subject terms, it is worthwhile to look at the applicable section of the file's alphabetical listing of terms or authors, if such is available, and to add to the search any apparent misspellings of the required term.

Hedgehopper is not a common name, but what about Thomas Edward Smith? There are many T. E. Smiths. Would there be more than one chemist named T. E. Smith? Probably. Would more than one T. E. Smith be working in the field of crown polymers? Possibly. But at least a narrowing down of results might be obtained by searching for

    SMITH, T. E. and POLYMER/ (truncated)

which would pick up documents by our friend Tom Smith, as well as by Ted, and Tim, but only those documents for which the term POLYMER/ appears or which were published in journals that have the word "polymer" in the title.

Another searchable surrogate, often included in the author field, is the author affiliation or the corporate source. Figure 3.7 shows how the affiliation appears in the July, 1979 CA Search from Chemical Abstracts as produced by the Lockheed DIALOG program (Inst. Anorg. Chem. Anal. Chem., Johannes Gutenberg-Univ., Mainz, Ger.) The corporate source is often valuable in pinpointing exact information. For many searches it is wise to restrict the corporate source aspect to the appropriate field in order to eliminate from the results information about rather than from the corporate source.

Journal Names and Dates

Journal names and dates are also viable entry points. A searcher may wish to locate an article which appeared in Chemical and Engineering News in 1977 on the subject of nuclear wastes. Much has been published about nuclear wastes, so restricting the search to Chemical and Engineering News is worthwhile. Certainly, even in Chemical and Engineering News for 1977, there will be more than one article on nuclear wastes. But the list resulting from the search should identify for the searcher the particular article he is looking for, and perhaps also bring to his attention other articles of interest.

Journal names are entered in different files in different ways. Standardization of journal references is greatly to be desired [9]. The use of

---

CA09021168687M
    Pentakis(dimethyltin) diphosphide, structure and nuclear magnetic resonance spectra of tin-rich bicyclic compound
    Author: Mathiasch, B.
    Location: Inst. Anorg. Chem. Anal. Chem., Johannes Gutenberg-Univ., Mainz, Ger.
    Section: CA029008   Publ Class: JOURNAL
    Journal: J. Organomet. Chem.   Coden: JORCAI   Publ: 79
    Series: 165   Issue: 3   Pages: 295-301   Language: Ger
    Identifiers: tin pentakisdimethyl diphosphide structure, diphosphapentastannabicycloheptane, NMR diphosphapentastannabicycloheptane

CA09021168687M
    Descriptors: Crystal structure; Molecular structure
    Identifiers: decamethyldiphosphapentastannabicycloheptane
    CAS Registry Numbers: 67761-26-6

Figure 3.7 Example item from CA Search file. (Material reprinted from Chemical Abstracts Service publications and services is copyrighted by the American Chemical Society and is reproduced with permission. No further copying is permitted.)

Entry Points

the American Chemical Society's CODEN is most helpful, and on all files where it is possible the CODEN should be used for the journal name. Figure 3.8 gives a partial list of CODENs [10].

The <u>New York Times</u> file also identifies journals by a set of alphabetics. Figure 3.9 shows a listing issued in 1979. Updated versions may be obtained from The Information Bank, Suite 86035, One World Trade Center, New York, NY 10048.

Numerical Data

Numerical data are searchable in some bibliographic files. When numerical data are the goal of the search, recourse to strictly data files, where available, is recommended. See [2] in Chap. 2. For files which contain numerical data, numeric codes, or digital codes, these codes are used as are ordinary alphabetic search (or index) terms. Figure 3.10 illustrates such numerical search terms. If a program includes a greater than—less than capability, the file is usually a strictly data file.

Chemical Structure

Chemical structure is often a useful entry for a chemical search [11,12]. A specific entry to a known chemical compound is the CAS registry number, where available. The registry number results from a method developed by the Chemical Abstracts Service by which every chemical is assigned a permanent, unique, computer-checkable registry number which identifies the substance within the CAS data base. Registry numbers are now included on the CA Search tapes (Fig. 3.7). Figure 3.11 gives an example page from the July-December 1976 <u>Chemical Abstracts Chemical Substance Index</u>. The registry numbers appear within brackets in the form 5 digits-2 digits-1 digit. The registry number for 1-Butanaminium,4-carboxy-N,N,N-trimethylhydroxide is [6778-33-2].

Another search program capability used for chemical structure searching is "truncation"—the use of a piece of a word, or stem, to pick up a number of similar words. "-CARBO-" would pick up CARBOXY within a name, as in the chemical compound above; and also DICARBOXY, CARBON, BICARBONATE, CARBONLESS, CARBOLIC, etc.

Truncating is useful for reducing the number of terms that must be specified. PREVENT-, where the hyphen is a sign meaning any term beginning with "PREVENT," will pick up PREVENT, PREVENTABLE, PREVENTION, PREVENTS, PREVENTIVE, and PREVENTIVENESS.

On some search programs, the number of letters which can be interchanged can be indicated as follows: PREVENT**** will pick up PREVENTABLE, PREVENTIVE, PREVENTION, PREVENTS, and PREVENT, but not PREVENTIVENESS. An example of an internal stem search (two stems with

LIST OF PERIODICALS

The List of Periodicals gives the CODEN and short journal title for each periodical covered by *Chemical Titles* in 1979. In each issue after the first of a given year, there will be published a cumulative list of all changes, additions, and deletions for the titles and CODEN for the journals on the 1979 *Chemical Titles* List of Periodicals.

CODEN	Title	CODEN	Title	CODEN	Title
ACHRE4	Acc. Chem. Res.	BJPCBM	Br. J. Pharmacol.	DMDSAI	Drug Metab. Dispos.	IJPPC3	Int. J. Pept. Protein Res.
ABPLAF	Acta Biochim. Pol.	BAPBAN	Bull. Acad. Pol. Sci.	ECSLA2	Earth Planet. Sci. Lett.	IJQCB2	Int. J. Quantum Chem.
ABMGAJ	Acta Biol. Med. Ger.		Ser. Sci. Biol.	EGLLA2	Econ. Geol.	IJQBDZ	Int. J. Quantum Chem.
ACAPCT	Acta Chem. Scand., Ser.	BAPCAQ	Bull. Acad. Pol. Sci.,	ENTKDR	Eesti NSV Tead. Akad.		Quantum Biol. Symp.
	A		Ser. Sci. Chim.		Toim. Keem.	IJQSDI	Int. J. Quantum Chem.
ACBOCV	Acta Chem. Scand., Ser.	BCSJA8	Bull. Chem. Soc. Jpn.	EGJCA3	Egypt. J. Chem.		Symp.
	B	BECTA6	Bull. Environ. Contam.	ELCAAV	Electrochim. Acta	IJRBA3	Int. J. Radiat. Biol.
ACASA2	Acta Chim. Acad. Sci.		Toxicol.	ELKKAX	Elektrokhimiya		Relat. Stud. Phys.
	Hung.	BICRAS	Bull. Inst. Chem. Res.,	EOBMAF	Elektron Obrab. Mater.		Chem. Med.
ACACBN	Acta Crystallogr., Sect.		Kyoto Univ.	EDRCAM	Endeavour	IJVNAP	Int. J. Vitam. Nutr. Res.
	A	BSCBAG	Bull. Soc. Chim. Belg.	ENDOAO	Endocrinology	INFZA9	Inzh.-Fiz. Zh.
ACBCAR	Acta Crystallogr., Sect.	BSCFAS	Bull. Soc. Chim. Fr.		(Philadelphia)	IJRIAC	Ital. J. Biochem.
	B	BUMPAK	Bum. Prom-st.	ENDKAC	Endokrinologie	ISJCAT	Isr. J. Chem.
ACENA7	Acta Endocrinol.	BNSKAK	Bunseki Kagaku	ESTHAG	Environ. Sci. Technol.	IKAKAK	Izv. Akad. Nauk Kaz.
	(Copenhagen)	BBMAE	Byull. Eksp. Biol. Med.	EKEPAB	Erdoel Kohle, Erdgas,		SSR, Ser. Khim.
ACEDAB	Acta Endocrinol.	CNREA8	Cancer Res.		Petrochem.	IZNMAQ	Izv. Akad. Nauk SSSR,
	(Copenhagen), Suppl.	CIBIAE	Carbohydr. Res.	EJBCAI	Eur. J. Biochem.		Met.
AHISA9	Acta Histochem.	CJCHAG	Can. J. Chem.	EJMCA5	Eur. J. Med. Chem.	IVNMAW	Izv. Akad. Nauk SSSR,
AHSUAV	Acta Histochem., Suppl.	CJCEA7	Can. J. Chem. Eng.		Chim. Ther.		Neorg. Mater.
AHCBAU	Acta Hydrochim.	CJMIAZ	Can. J. Microbiol.	EJPHAZ	Eur. J. Pharmacol.	IANBAM	Izv. Akad. Nauk SSSR,
	Hydrobiol.	CNJPA2	Can. J. Pharm. Sci.	EUPJAG	Eur. Polym. J.		Ser. Biol.
AMETAR	Acta Metall.	CJPHAD	Can. J. Phys.	EXCREAL	Exp. Cell Res.	IANFAY	Izv. Akad. Nauk SSSR,
APTOA6	Acta Pharmacol.	CJPPA3	Can. J. Physiol.	EXPEAM	Experientia		Ser. Fiz.
	Toxicol.		Pharmacol.	EXPSAU	Experientia, Suppl.	IANGA3	Izv. Akad. Nauk SSSR,
APTSAI	Acta Pharmacol.	CPLSAY	Can. J. Plant Sci.	EXPAAA	Exp. Parasitol.		Ser. Geol.
	Toxicol., Suppl.	CJSSAR	Can. J. Soil Sci.	FALAAA	Farbe Lack	IASKA6	Izv. Akad. Nauk SSSR,
APHCAO	Acta Pharm. Hung.	CJSPAI	Can. J. Spectrosc.	FRPPAO	Farmaco, Ed. Prat.		Ser. Khim.
APSXAS	Acta Pharm. Suec.	CAMIA6	Can. Mineral.	FRPSAX	Farmaco, Ed. Sci.	ITUFAW	Izv. Akad. Nauk Turkm.
ATPLB6	Acta Phys. Pol. A	CRBRAT	Carbohydr. Res.	FATOAO	Farmakol. Toksikol.		SSR, Ser. Fiz.-Tekh.
APOBBB	Acta Phys. Pol. B	CRBNAH	Carbon		(Moscow)		Khim. Geol. Nauk
APSCAX	Acta Physiol. Scand.	CELLB5	Cell	FRMTAL	Farmatsiya (Moscow)	IUZFAU	Izv. Akad. Nauk Uzb.
APSSAD	Acta Physiol. Scand.,	CLIMB8	Cell. Immunol.	FEBLAL	FEBS Lett.		SSR, Ser. Fiz.-Mat.
	Suppl.	CECHAF	Cereal Chem.	FUZKAP	Farm. Zh. (Kiev)		Nauk
ADCSAJ	Adv. Chem. Ser.	CKFRAY	Cesk. Farm.	FEPRA7	Fed. Proc. Fed. Am.	IZSKAB	Izv. Sib. Otd. Akad.
AGACBH	Agents Actions	CAMIAJ	Chem. Anal. (Warsaw)		Soc. Exp. Biol.		Nauk SSSR, Ser.
ABCHA6	Agric. Biol. Chem.	CHEBAM	Chem. Biol. Interact.	FSPMAM	Fermenta. Sport.		Khim. Nauk
AGRCAX	Agrochimica	CBNAR	Chem. Br.		Prom-st.	ITSAA7	Izv. Timryazevsk. S-kh.
AGKYAU	Agrokhimiya	CHMBAY	Chem. Eng. (N. Y.)	FERO48	Ferroelectrics		Akad.
AICEAC	AIChE J.	CHEEA3	Chem. Eng. Prog.	FSASAX	Fette, Seifen, Anstrichm.	IVUMAX	Izv. Vyssh. Uchebn.
ACSBA7	Am. Ceram. Soc., Bull.	CEPRA8	Chem. Eng. Sci.	FCMLAS	Finn. Chem. Lett.		Zaved. Chern.
AJPHAP	Am. J. Physiol.	CESCAC	Chem. Eng. (London)	FBKRAT	Fiziol. Biokhim. Kult.		Metall.
AJSCAP	Am. J. Sci.	CMERA9	Chem. Eng. (London)		Rast.	IVUFAC	Izv. Vyssh. Uchebn.
AMMJAY	Am. Mineral.	CHGEAD	Chem. Geol.	FZRSAV	Fiziol. Rast.		Zaved., Fiz.
ANBCA2	Anal. Biochem.	CHINAG	Chem. Ind. (London)	FIZHDO	Fiziol. Zh. (Kiev)	IVUKAR	Izv. Vyssh. Uchebn.
ANCHAM	Anal. Chem.	CITEAH	Chem. Ing. Tech.	FZLZAM	Fiziol. Zh. SSSR im. I.		
ACACAM	Anal. Chim. Acta	CHRYAO	Chemistry		M. Sechenova		

Entry Points

CODEN	Journal
ANALBP	Anal. Lett.
ANLSCY	Analusis
ANALAO	Analyst (London)
ANFIA6	An. Fis.
ANCEAD	Angew. Chem.
ANMCBO	Angew. Makromol. Chem.
ANQUBU	An. Quim.
ANCPAC	Ann. Chim. (Paris)
ANIMCZ	Ann. Immunol. (Paris)
ANMBCM	Ann. Microbiol. (Paris)
APHAA9	Ann. N. Y. Acad. Sci.
APTRAD	Ann. Pharm. Fr.
ANFYA2	Ann. Phys. (Leipzig)
APNYA6	Ann. Phys. (N.Y.)
ANTBAL	Antibiotiki (Moscow)
AMACCQ	Antimicrob. Agents Chemother.
AEMIDF	Appl. Environ. Microbiol.
APHYCC	Appl. Phys. Lett.
APPSAB	Appl. Polym. Symp.
APSPAX	Appl. Spectrosc.
APSPA2	Astrophys. J. Suppl. Ser.
AENGAB	At. Energ.
ATENBP	Atmos. Environ.
AJBSAM	Aust. J. Biol. Sci.
AJCHAS	Aust. J. Chem.
BBPCAX	Ber. Bunsenges. Phys. Chem.
BBRCA9	Biochem. Biophys. Res. Commun.
BIGEBA	Biochem. Genet.
BICHAW	Biochemistry
BIOAK6	Biochem. Med.
BIMDA2	Biochem. Pharmacol.
BCPCA6	Biochem. Soc. Trans.
BBACBS	Biochim. Biophys. Acta
BICMBE	Biochimie
BIOFAI	Biofizika
BICHBX	Bioinorg. Chem.
BIOHAO	Biokhimiya (Moscow)
BKCMBM	Bioorg. Chem.
BIKHD7	Bioorg. Khim.
BICJAZ	Biophys. Chem.
BIPMAA	Biophys. J.
BIPLBS	Biopolymers
BIRLAU	Biotechnol. Bioeng.
BTMNA7	Biuletyn
BCFAAI	Bull. Chim. Farm.
BRREAP	Brain Res.
BJCAAI	Br. J. Cancer
CMLTAG	Chem. Lett.
CHLSAC	Chem. Listy
CPSHAF	Chemsphere
CPBTAL	Chem. Pharm. Bull.
CMPHC2	Chem. Phys.
CHPLBC	Chem. Phys. Lett.
CPLIA4	Chem. Phys. Lipids
CHREAY	Chem. Prum.
CSRVBR	Chem. Rev.
CHSWAP	Chem. Soc. Rev.
CHTEDD	Chem. Stosow.
CHTEAA	CHEMTECH
CMKZAT	Chem. Tech. (Leipzig)
CHIMAD	Chim. Ind. (Milan)
CHRGB7	Chromatographia
CIRUAL	Circ. Res.
CIRSAF	Circ. Res., Suppl.
CLCMAB	Clays Clay Miner.
CLCHAU	Clin. Chem. (Winston Salem. N. C.)
CCATAR	Clin. Chim. Acta
CLPTAT	Clin. Pharmacol. Ther.
CSMMCA	Clin. Sci. Mol. Med.
CCCCAK	Collect. Czech. Chem. Commun.
CPMSB6	Colloid Polym. Sci.
CBFMAO	Combust. Flame
CBPAB5	Comp. Biochem. Physiol. A
CBPBB8	Comp. Biochem. Physiol. B
CBPCBB	Comp. Biochem. Physiol. C
CMPEAP	Contrib. Mineral. Petrol.
CCHRAM	Coord. Chem. Rev.
CORRAK	Corrosion (Houston)
CRRSAA	Corros. Sci.
CHDBAN	C. R. Hebd. Seances Acad. Sci., Ser. B
CHDDAT	C. R. Hebd. Seances Acad. Sci., Ser. C
CCACAA	C. R. Hebd. Seances Acad. Sci., Ser. D
CRSBAW	Croat. Chem. Acta
CRSBAW	C. R. Seances Soc. Biol. Ses Fil.
CRYOAX	Cryogenics
CSCMCS	Cryst. Struct. Commun.
DKOKAZ	Denki Kagaku Oyobi Kogyo Butsuri Kagaku
DANAAW	Dokl. Akad. Nauk Arm. SSR
DBLRAC	Dokl. Akad. Nauk B. SSR
DANKAS	Dokl. Akad. Nauk SSSR
DANTAL	Dokl. Akad. Nauk Tadzh. SSR
DRANAD	Dopov. Akad. Nauk Ukr. RSR, Ser. B: Geol., Khim. Biol. Nauki
DANND6	
FKMMAJ	Fiz. Khim. Mekh. Mater.
FKOMAT	Fiz. Khim. Obrab. Mater.
FMMTAK	Fiz. Met. Metalloved.
FTPPA4	Fiz. Tekh. Poluprovodn. (Leningrad)
FTVTAC	Fiz. Tverd. Tela (Leningrad)
FCTXAV	Food Cosmet. Toxicol.
ZACFAU	Fresenius' Z. Anal. Chem.
FUELAC	Fuel
GCTTA9	Gazz. Chim. Ital.
GCENAS	Gen. Comp. Endocrinol.
GKOGAM	Genshiryoku Kyoyo
GCACAK	Geochim. Cosmochim. Acta
GCASD3	Geochim. Cosmochim. Acta, Suppl.
GEOKAQ	Geokhimiya
GEZHA4	Geol. Zh. (Russ. Ed.)
GLKPA2	Gidroliz. Lesokhim. Prom-st.
GISAAA	Gig. Sanit.
HKOKDE	Hakko Kogaku Kaishi
HAKOD4	Hakko To Kogyo
HCACAV	Helv. Chim. Acta
HPACAK	Helv. Phys. Acta
HPYSAI	Helv. Phys. Acta, Suppl.
HTCYAM	Heterocycles
HITSAC	High Temp. Sci.
HCMYAL	Histochemistry
HSZPAZ	Hoppe-Seyler's Z. Physiol. Chem.
HMMRA2	Horm. Metab. Res.
HRMRA3	Horm. Res.
HYINDN	Hyperfine Interact.
IEJQA7	IEEE J. Quantum Electron.
IETNAE	IEEE Trans. Nucl. Sci.
IMCHAZ	Immunochemistry
IMMUAM	Immunology
IECFA7	Ind. Eng. Chem., Fundam.
IEPDAW	Ind. Eng. Chem., Process. Des. Dev.
IEPRA6	Ind. Eng. Chem., Prod. Res. Dev.
IJBBBQ	Indian J. Biochem. Biophys.
IJCADU	Indian J. Chem., Sect. A
IJSBDB	Indian J. Chem., Sect. B
IJEBA6	Indian J. Exp. Biol.
IJPSDW	Indian J. Pharm. Sci.
IJPAU	Indian J. Pure Appl. Phys.
INOCAJ	Inorg. Chem.
ICHAA3	Inorg. Chim. Acta
INUCAF	Inorg. Nucl. Chem. Lett.
IJARAY	Int. J. Appl. Radiat. Isot.
IJBOBV	Int. J. Biochem.
IJCKBO	Int. J. Chem. Kinet.
IJMIBY	Int. J. Mass Spectrom. Ion Phys.
IVUNA2	Izv. Vyssh. Uchebn. Zaved., Neft Gaz
IVUPA8	Izv. Vyssh. Uchebn. Zaved., Pishch. Tekhnol.
IVUTAK	Izv. Vyssh. Uchebn. Zaved., Tsvetn. Metall.
JAFCAU	J. Agric. Food Chem.
JACTAW	J. Am. Ceram. Soc.
JACSAT	J. Am. Chem. Soc.
JAOCA7	J. Am. Oil Chem. Soc.
JAWWA5	J. Am. Water Works Assoc.
JANSAG	J. Anim. Sc.
JANTAJ	J. Antibiot.
JIAPAS	Jpn. J. Appl. Phys.
JACBBD	J. Appl. Chem. Biotechnol.
JACGAR	J. Appl. Crystallogr.
JAELBJ	J. Appl. Electrochem.
JAPIAU	J. Appl. Phys.
JAPNAB	J. Appl. Polym. Sci.
JANCA2	J. Assoc. Off. Anal. Chem.
JOBAAY	J. Bacteriol.
JOBIAO	J. Biochem. (Tokyo)
JBCHA3	J. Biol. Chem.
JCNNAF	J. Carbohydr., Nucleosides, Nucleotides
JCTLA5	J. Catal.
JCLBA3	J. Cell Biol.
JCEDA8	J. Chem. Educ.
JCEAAX	J. Chem. Eng. Data
JCEJAQ	J. Chem. Eng. Jpn.
JCISD8	J. Chem. Inf. Comput. Sci.
JCPSA6	J. Chem. Phys.
JRPSDC	J. Chem. Res. (S)
JCCCAT	J. Chem. Soc., Chem. Commun.
JCDTBI	J. Chem. Soc., Dalton Trans.
JCFTAR	J. Chem. Soc., Faraday Trans. 1
JCFTBS	J. Chem. Soc., Faraday Trans. 2
JCPRB4	J. Chem. Soc., Perkin Trans. 1
JCPKBH	J. Chem. Soc., Perkin Trans. 2
JCTDAF	J. Chem. Thermodyn.
JCPBAN	J. Chim. Phys. Phys.-Chim. Biol.
JCCTAC	J. Chin. Chem. Soc. (Taipei)
JOCRAM	J. Chromatogr. Sci.
JCHSRZ	Chromatogr. Sci.
JCCBDT	J. Clin. Chem. Clin. Biochem.
JCEMAZ	J. Clin. Endocrinol. Metab.
JCINAO	J. Clin. Invest.

Figure 3.8 Partial list of journal CODENs. (Taken from Chemical Titles, 1979. Material reprinted from Chemical Abstracts Service publications and services is copyrighted by the American Chemical Society and is reproduced with permission. No further copying is permitted.)

NYT	- NEW YORK TIMES	LAE	- LATIN AMERICA ECONOMIC REPORT
AA	- ADVERTISING AGE	LAM	- LATIN AMERICA POLITICAL REPORT
AB	- AMERICAN BANKER		
AC	- ATLANTA CONSTITUTION	LAT	- LOS ANGELES TIMES
AMN	- AMSTERDAM NEWS	LF	- LIFE
AS	- AMERICAN SCHOLAR	LK	- LOOK
AST	- ASTRONAUTICS	LOB	- LONDON OBSERVER
ATL	- ATLANTIC MONTHLY	LST	- LONDON SUNDAY TIMES
ATS	- ATLAS		
AUT	- AUTOMOTIVE NEWS	MCL	- McCALLS
AW	- AVIATION WEEK AND SPACE TECHNOLOGY	ME	- MIDDLE EAST
		MG	- MANCHESTER GUARDIAN
		MH	- MIAMI HERALD
BAS	- BULLETIN OF ATOMIC SCIENTISTS	MND	- LE MONDE
		MTR	- MANHATTAN TRIBUNE
BLS	- BLACK SCHOLAR		
BLW	- BLACK WORLD	NDY	- NEWSDAY
BRN	- BARRONS	NJL	- NATIONAL JOURNAL
BW	- BUSINESS WEEK	NOB	- NATIONAL OBSERVER
		NRB	- NEW YORK REVIEW OF BOOKS
CB	- CURRENT BIOGRAPHY	NRP	- NEW REPUBLIC
CFT	- FINANCIAL TIMES (CANADA)	NRV	- NATIONAL REVIEW
CHD	- CHICAGO DEFENDER	NTN	- NATION (THE)
CMT	- COMMENTARY	NWK	- NEWSWEEK
CMW	- COMMONWEAL	NY	- NEW YORK
CR	- CONSUMERS REPORTS	NYR	- NEW YORKER
CSM	- CHRISTIAN SCIENCE MONITOR		
CT	- CHICAGO TRIBUNE	PCR	- PITTSBURGH COURIER
		PSY	- PSYCHOLOGY TODAY
EAP	- EDITOR AND PUBLISHER		
EBY	- EBONY	RD	- READERS DIGEST
ECL	- ECONOMIST OF LONDON	RMP	- RAMPARTS
EJ	- EDMONTON JOURNAL		
		SAM	- SCIENTIFIC AMERICAN
FEE	- FAR EASTERN ECONOMIC REVIEW	SCI	- SCIENCE
		SFC	- SAN FRANCISCO CHRONICLE
FIN	- FINANCIAL TIMES OF LONDON	SIL	- SPORTS ILLUSTRATED
		SPT	- SPORT
FP	- FOREIGN POLICY	SR	- SATURDAY REVIEW
FRB	- FORBES		
FRN	- FOREIGN AFFAIRS	TDY	- TUESDAY
FTN	- FORTUNE	TM	- TIME
		TL	- TIMES OF LONDON
HBR	- HARVARD BUSINESS REVIEW	TS	- TORONTO STAR
HC	- HOUSTON CHRONICLE		
HRP	- HARPERS	USN	- US NEWS AND WORLD REPORT
IND	- INDUSTRIAL RESEARCH	VG	- VOGUE
		VTY	- VARIETY
JCM	- JOURNAL OF COMMERCE	VV	- VILLAGE VOICE
JET	- JET		
		WMY	- WASHINGTON MONTHLY
		WP	- WASHINGTON POST
		WSJ	- WALL STREET JOURNAL
		WWD	- WOMENS WEAR DAILY

Figure 3.9 Abbreviations for publications indexed in the New York Times Information Bank. (Reproduced with permission.)

Entry Points 47

PREDICASTS FILE
EIS PLANTS

DIGITAL CODES WHICH CAN BE USED FOR SEARCH AND SORT:

    INDUSTRY (SIC) CODE
    SALES (MIL $)
    HDQTRS ZIP
    HDQTRS CODE
    EMPLOYMENT SIZE CLASS
    SHARE OF MARKET
    GEOGRAPHIC CODE
    BRANCH ZIP

Figure 3.10 Numerical surrogates for Predicasts EIS Plants. (Reproduced with permission by Predicasts, Inc.)

a specified number of replaceable characters between them) is POLY*MIDE for POLYAMIDE or POLYIMIDE.

Left-hand truncation is much more difficult to program than right-hand, and therefore much more expensive. Left-hand truncation is of great value in chemical searching, however. For instance, *BENZOIN will cover BENZOIN ETHER, DIAKYLAMINOBENZOIN, AMINOBENZOIN, METHYL BENZOIN CROSSLINKING CATALYST, BENZOIN ALKOXYCARBONYL ETHER, METHOXYCARBONYLBENZOIN, POLYBENZOIN, BENZOIN POLYOL ETHER, HYDROXYMETHYLBENZOIN, and other derivatives.

While stem or truncation searching is an adjunct to skillful searching, especially on the chemical files, great care should be exercised. Stems of three characters or less are seldom advisable. As a matter of fact, even an untruncated search term of three characters or less can lead to trouble. More than one searcher has used the chemical symbol for calcium, Ca, in the free-text mode on the Chemical Abstracts file, only to be rewarded by every abstract in the file up to the fail-safe cutoff number. Figure 3.7 is an example of a Chemical Abstracts file item in which CA, meaning Chemical Abstracts, appears in the searchable field containing the section number.

Examination of posting dictionaries, permuted listings in thesauri, and keyword in context (KWIC) indexes such as Chemical Titles [13], will show what will be retrieved by a given word stem. An example is shown in Fig. 3.12.

Chemical information is often best communicated by describing the fragments making up the chemical molecule, or by graphics showing the positions of functional groups in the chemical molecule. Several efforts have been made to set up a search method for chemical files based on molecular structure. Some of these are the Wiswesser Line Notation [12], the Chemical-Biological Coordination Center Code 22 [14], and connectivity

1093CS

—, N,3,3-trimethyl-2-methylene-N-2-propenyl-conjugate acid [60400-61-5], radical cyclization of, 122976y
—, N,3,3-trinitro-
  lithium salt [59263-90-0], prepn. and reaction with ferrocenylmethylpyridinium tosylate, 5845u
1-Butan-3-d-amine
— 3-methyl- [60111-17-3]
  deamination of, mechanism of, 77156t
2-Butanamine (sec-butylamine) [13952-84-6]
  addn. reaction with dichlorovinylamides, 45932b
  amination by, of benzyl chloride or chloromethylated polystyrene, kinetics of, solvent effect on, 143769y
  amination of dihalobutenes with, 159300z
  N-carbonylation of, initiators for, 123292j
  catalytic efficiency of, for conversion of butyl bromide to butyl cyanide, 20581y
  Ceratocystis ulmi control by, 105217j
  conductometric titration of benzoic acid nitro derivs. with, in methyl salicylate, 142442z
  of cooked chicken volatiles, 107577a
  core binding energy and proton affinity of, 45829y
  cyclization with acetamidodichloroacrylonitrile, 177295f
  detn. of
    chloranil in spectrophotometric, 171312n
    in formulations and residues, R 105133d
  detn. of enantiomeric purity of optically active, NMR shift reagents for, P 28341r
  effect of, on nickel-catalyzed dimerization of isoprene, 4784m
  insect attractant contg., for eye gnat, 42166u
  with isoquinolinium salts, 106853z
  luminescence of lanthanide shift reagent in presence of, 133513w
  in meteorite Murchison, Australia, 97203j
  potato growth and yield response to, 138834t
  radiolysis of rigid org. glasses contg., trapped electron and anion formation in, 134121d
  reaction of
    with aluminum, 71499k
    with chloroacetic acid, 136376q
    with chloroacetoxylidide, P 56896b
    with 4-chloro-5,7-dinitro-2-(trifluoromethyl)benzimidazole, P 94361y
    with dichlorodinitrobenzotrifluoride, P 142756q
    with dichloroxanthene deriv., P 110104z
    with dihydromethanoanthrylpropionaldehydes, P 62865z
  with ethyl (alkylsulfonyl)hoxamates, 93767y
  with guanyl thiourea deriv., P 159475k
  with pyridinedicarboximides, P 142990b
  reaction with benzaldehyde, salicylaldehyde, or nickel(bisalicylaldehyde), kinetics of, 20286f
  reaction with benzaldehyde and Grignard reagents, 137174j
  reaction with chloroacetoxylidide, P 87545h
  reductive condensation of, with methyl isobutyl ketone, P 176815p
  (R)- [13250-12-9], core binding energy and proton affinity of, 45829y
  (S)- [513-49-5], core binding energy and proton affinity of, 45829y

JULY-DEC. 1976 CHEM. SUBSTANCE INDEX

  of, P 77855v
—, N,N-dimethyl-1-[[1-(phenylmethyl)-1H-indazol-3-yl]oxy]- [59946-32-5], P 69062x
—, N-[(diphenyl)phosphinothioyl)thio]- [60073-91-1], 160253t
—, N,N-dipropyl- [60421-91-2]
  gas chromatog. of, substituent effect on retention index of, 77539v
—, N-methyl- [7713-69-1], P 176815p
  amination of ketones by, reductive, P 62629a
—, 2-methyl- (tert-pentylamine) [594-39-8]
  reaction of
    with chloroacetic acid, 136376q
    with 4-chloro-5,7-dinitro-2-(trifluoromethyl)benzimidazole, P 94361y
—, N-methyl-N-nitroso- [35606-37-2]
  detn. of, 104730j
—, N-(1-methylpropyl)- [626-23-3]
  reaction of, with dimethylaminooxathiazolanes, 21232x
  reaction with ethylthiophosphine sulfide and tricyclohexyltin chloride, P 46851t
—, N-(2-methylpropyl)- [39190-88-0], P 176815p
—, 1-[[1-(phenylmethyl)-1H-indazol-3-yl]oxy]- [42945-16-4], P 63062x
1-Butanaminium
—, 2-acetyl-4-cyano-N,N,N-trimethyl-
  iodide [10590-54-2], reaction of, with (methylenedioxy)dihydroisoquinoline, 63207y
—, N-[2-(acetyloxy)ethyl]-N,N-diethyl- [54322-46-2]
  acetylcholinesterase reaction with methanesulfonyl fluoride response to, 58734p
—, N-[2-(acetyloxy)ethyl]-N,N-dimethyl- [54322-45-1]
  acetylcholinesterase reaction with methanesulfonyl fluoride response to, 58734p
  bromide [60037-46-9], hydrolysis of, by cholinesterase, 58735q
—, 2-(acetyloxy)-4-methoxy-N,N,N-trimethyl-4-oxo-
  bromide, (R)- [61043-60-3], parasympathomimetic activity and toxicity of, 186608n
  bromide, (S)- [61042-99-7], parasympathomimetic activity and toxicity of, 186608n
—, 4-(acetylthio)-N,N,N-trimethyl-
  iodide [24578-80-1], cattle tick acetylcholinesterase specificity for, 58013c
—, 4-(boryloxy)-N,N,N-trimethyl-4-oxo-
  hexafluorophosphate(1-), compd. with N,N-dimethylmethanamine (1:1) [58815-65-9], 40220h
—, 3-[(4-butoxybenzoyl)oxy]-N,N,N-triethyl-2-methyl-
  iodide [3818-40-4], heart metab. response to, in cardiac insufficiency, 56816t
—, N-butyl-N-[9-(2-carboxyphenyl)-6-(dibutylamino)-3H-xanthen-3-ylidene]-
  chloride [7083-23-0], laser soln. contg. diphenylbutadiene, 200367s
—, N-butyl-N-[6-(dibutylamino)-9-[2,4-disulfophenyl]-3H-xanthen-3-ylidene]-
  hydroxide, inner salt, sodium salt [60655-69-8], P 134053h

48 The Strategy of Mechanized Search

Consult Vol. 76-85 Cumulative Index Guide Before Using This Index

  trichloro-tartrate(1-) [59686-76-9], catalysts, for prepn. of dimethyltin dichloride from tin and methyl chloride, P 33187z
—, N,N-dibutyl-N-(1-methylethyl)-
  fluoride [64-35-98-5], systems, water-, 113162c
—, N,N-dibutyl-N-(2-methylpropyl)-
  fluoride [60-26-67-0], systems, water-, 113162c
—, N,N-dibutyl-N-propyl-
  fluoride [64-33-97-4], systems, water-, 113162c
—, N,N-diethyl-2,3-bis(hydroxyimino)-N-oxo-
  methyl- [60253-88-5]
  protonation of, solvent effect on, 108179j
—, N,N-diethyl-N-[3-[(ethylcarbonimidoyl)-amino]propyl]-4-sulfo-
  hydroxide, inner salt [59457-33-9], photog. hardening agent, P 12299x
—, N,N-diethyl-N-(2-hydroxyethyl)- [54322-49-5]
  acetylcholinesterase reaction with methanesulfonyl fluoride response to, 58734p
—, N,N-diethyl-2-(hydroxyimino)-N-methyl-3-oxo- [60253-87-4]
  protonation of solvent effect on, 108179j
—, N,N-diethyl-N-[3-[(methylcarbonimidoyl)amino]propyl]-4-sulfo-
  hydroxide, inner salt [59457-32-8], photog. hardening agent, P 12299x
—, N,N-dimethyl-N-[3-[(methylcarbonimidoyl)amino]propyl]-4-sulfo-
  hydroxide, inner salt [57542-83-3], photog. hardening agent, P 12299x
—, N,N-dimethyl-N-[3-[[(1-methylethyl)carbonimidoyl]amino]propyl]-4-sulfo-
  hydroxide, inner salt [59457-30-6], photog. hardening agent, P 12299x
—, 1-[[(6,9-dimethyl-3-(1-methylethyl)-7-(2-methylpropyl)-5,8-dioxo-2-oxa-6,9-diazabicyclo[10.2.2]hexadeca-10,12,14,15-tetraen-4-yl]methylamino]carbonyl]-N,N,2-tetramethyl-
  iodide, [3R-[3R*,4S*(2S*,3S*),7S*]]- [54864-47-0]
  prepn. and conformation of, 108871d
—, 4-ethoxy-2-hydroxy-N,N,N-trimethyl-4-oxo-
  bromide, (+)- [17548-19-7], parasympathomimetic activity and toxicity of, 186608n
  bromide, (R)- [51847-35-9], parasympathomimetic activity and toxicity of, 186608n
—, N-[2-[(ethylcarbonimidoyl)amino]propyl]-N,N-dimethyl-4-sulfo-
  hydroxide, inner salt [59457-41-9], photog. hardening agent, P 12299x
—, N-[3-[(ethylcarbonimidoyl)amino]propyl]-N,N-dimethyl-4-sulfo-
  hydroxide, inner salt [57542-84-4], photog. hardening agent, P 12299x
—, 2-ethyl-N,N,N-trimethyl-3-oxo-

aluminum complex [53923-20-9], 71499k
cobalt complex, (S)- [59930-78-8], CD and mol.
  symmetry of, 26889c
compd. with 2,3,5,6-tetrachloro-2,5-=
  cyclohexadiene-1,4-dione (1:1) [60731-43-3],
  spectrum and stability const. of, 171312n
5-(2,4-dichlorophenoxy)-2-nitrobenzoate
  [53775-(?)-2], herbicidal activity of, P
  192391r
(dithio ... arbodithioato-S,S')[(1,2-=
  ethane iy)bis(carbamodithioato)](2-)]=
  manganate(1-) [61301-41-5], prepn. and
  fungicidal activity of, P 192194r
(T-4)-[dimethylcarbamodithioato-S,S'][(1,2-=
  ethanediylbis(carbamodithioato)](2-)]=
  zincate(1-) [61061-11-8], prepn. and
  fungicidal activity of, P 192194r
diphenylphosphinodithioate [60732-02-7], 160253t
hydrochloride [10049-80-0]
  reaction of, with tetrahydrobenzothienyl
  isocyanates, P 32825x
  reaction with dithiocarbamates and metal salts, P
  192194r
hydrochloride, (S)- [31519-50-3], fungicidal action
  of, 172236t, 172237d
reaction products with epoxy resins, coatings,
  chem.-resistant, crosslinking of, by
  polyisocyanates, P 194234g
—, 1-[(5-chloro-1-(phenylmethyl)-1H-=
  indazol-3-yl)oxy]- [59920-68-2], P 63604x
—, 1-[(5-chloro-1-(phenylmethyl)-1H-=
  indazol-3-yl)oxy]-N,N-dimethyl-
  [59920-69-3], P 63604x
—, N,N-diethyl- [3422-60-1]
—, N,N-diethyl- [4358-75-2]
  deamination of, solvent effect in, 142219g
—, 3,3-dimethyl- [3850-30-4]
  deamination of, solvent effect in, 142219g
  reaction of, with 4-chloro-5,7-dinitro-2-=
  (trifluoromethyl)benzimidazole, P 94361y
  reaction with ethylthiophosphine sulfide and
  tricyclohexyltin chloride, P 46857t
  reaction products with glycidyl methacrylate,
  sealants, anaerobic, P 48472n
—, N-(1,1-dimethylethyl)-
  hydrochloride [60565-41-6], 122715n
—, 1-(2,6-dimethylphenoxy)-
  hydrochloride [29238-43-5], prepn. and
  anticonvulsant and antiarrhythmic properties
  of, P 77855v
—, 1-(2,6-dimethylphenoxy)-3-methyl-
  hydrochloride [29361-41-9], prepn. and
  anticonvulsant and antiarrhythmic properties

—, N-butyl-N-[6-(dibutylamino)-9-[2-=
  sulfophenyl)-3H-xanthen-3-ylidene]-
  hydroxide, inner salt [60530-10-1], lasers, P
  13405h
—, N-[6-(butylmethylamino)-9-[2-=
  carboxyphenyl)-3H-xanthen-3-yliden=
  e]-N-methyl-
  chloride [61192-55-0], laser soln. cont.
  1,4-diphenylbutadiene, 20036f's
—, N-butyl-3-methyl-N,N-bis(3-methylbutyl)-
  [21570-53-6]
  elec. cond. of, in cyclic ureas, 167536w
  iodide [5709-78-4]
  elec. cond. of, in cyclic ureas, 167536w
  elec. cond. of, in methylsulfolane, 16:534u
  tetraphenylborate(1-) [16742-92-0]
  elec. cond. of, in cyclic ureas, 167536w
  elec. cond. of, in methylsulfolane, 167534u
—, N-butyl-N-methyl-N-[2-(trimethylsilyl)=
  ethyl]-
  iodide [60323-01-5], prepn. and anionic
  rearrangement of, 108705e
—, N-butyl-N-(3-phenyl-2-propynyl-N-2-=
  propynyl-
  bromide [55998-24-2], base catalyzed intramol.
  cyclization of, 77965f
—, 4-carboxy-N,N,N-trimethyl-
  hydroxide, inner salt [6778-33-2], dielectric
  increments and conformation of, 108971m
—, N-[3-[(cyclohexyl)carbonimidoyl]amino]=
  propyl]-N,N-dimethyl-4-sulfo-
  hydroxide, inner salt [59457-34-0], photog.
  hardening agent, P 12299x
—, N-[3-[(cyclohexylcarbonimidoyl]amino]=
  propyl]-N,N-dimethyl-4-sulfo-
  hydroxide, inner salt [59457-31-7], photog.
  hardening agent, P 12299x
—, N,N-dibutyl-N-[2,5-diethoxyphenyl)=
  sulfonyl]
  chloride [60740-28-5], corrosion inhibitors, for steel
  in petroleum wells, 163069y

iodide [6535-61-7], cyclocondensation reaction with
  dihydroisoquinoline deriv. 124211u
—, 4-(hexadecyloxy)-2-hydroxy-N,N,N-=
  trimethyl-4-oxo-
  (R)- [16725-56-7], oxidn. of, by mitochondria of
  liver. ethanol inhibition of, aspartate and
  malate metab. in relation to, 172863e
—, N-(2-hydroxyethyl)-N,N-dimethyl-
  [35697-71-3]
  acetylcholinesterase reaction with methanesulfonyl
  fluoride response to, 58734p
—, 2-hydroxy-4-methoxy-N,N,N-trimethyl-=
  4-oxo-
  bromide, (R)- [33620-52-9], parasympathomimetic
  activity and toxicity of, 186608n
  bromide, (S)- [61042-98-6], parasympathomimetic
  activity and toxicity of, 186608n
—, 4-hydroxy-N,N,N-trimethyl-
  nitrite (salt) [6977-53-4], in froth flotation of ores, P
  186625u
—, 2-methyl-N,N,N-tris(2-methylbutyl)-
  salt with 2,4,6-trinitrophenol (1:1) [55482-33-2]
  d. and viscosity of molten, near glass transition
  temp, 165482h
  elec. cond. of molten, near glass transition temp,
  165549c
—, 3-methyl-N,N,N-tris(3-methylbutyl)-
  [37541-17-1]
  triiodide formation of oxidized cholesterol
  membranes in presence of, 1492d
—, N,N,3-tetramethyl-3-[(1-oxo-2-=
  propenyl)amino]-
  chloride, homopolymer [42850-40-8], fractionation
  of, by Amberlite resins contg. quaternary
  ammonium chloride functions, P 7904r
  methyl sulfate [55554-65-9], manuf. of, for dye
  assistants and flocculating agents, P 144248q
  methyl sulfate, polymer with 2-propenamide
  [57177-57-2], manuf. of, for dye assistants and
  flocculating agents, P 144248q
—, N,N,N-tributyl- [10549-76-5]
  activity and diffusion of protons in presence of aq.
  solns. of, 25485e
  adsorption of, by platinum, photoelec. emission in
  relation to, 200032d
  anion polarog. redn. in presence of, current min. in
  relation to, 132775z
  detection of, by thin-layer chromatog., 88113c
  dipole interaction energy of, in various solvents,
  131452b
  in electrohydrodimerization, of amide or ester or
  nitrile, P 113811p
  free energy of transfer of
  from water to aq. acetonitrile soln., cavity effect
  in relation to, 192006f
  from water to dichloroethane, 10918z

Figure 3.11 Partial page from CAS Chemical Substance Index July-December 1976. (Material reprinted from Chemical Abstracts Service publications and services is copyrighted by the American Chemical Society and is reproduced with permission. No further copying is permitted.)

CAP* used to cover	CAP, CAPS, CAPPING	
TERMS which will hit on	CAP*	
CAP	CAPITAL	
CAPACITANCE	CAPROATES	
CAPACITOR	CAPROIC	
CAPACITY	CAPROLACTAM	
CAPILLARIES	CAPRYLIC	
CAPILLARY	CAPS	
CAPPING	CAPSULES	
RES* used to cover both	RESEARCH and	RES
TERMS which will hit on	RES*	
RES	RESIDUES	RESOURCES
RESCUE	RESILIENCE	RESPIRATION
RESEARCH	RESIN	RESPIRATORY
RESERPINE	RESISTANCE	RESPONSE
RESERVES	RESISTIVITY	RESTARTABLE
RESERVOIR	RESISTORS	RESTORING
RESET	RESNATRONS	RESTRAINING
RESETTLEMENT	RESOLUTION	REST
RESIDENTIAL	RESOLVING POWER	RESULFURIZED
RESIDUAL	RESONANCE	RESURFACING
	RESORCINOLS	RESUSCITATION

Figure 3.12   Examples of retrievals from three letter stems.

tables [11]. An excellent discussion of the ramifications of searching by structural fragments has been written by Garfield, Granito, and Petrarca [15]. A method of substructure searching has been developed by Farmer [16] of the CAS staff, which makes it possible to search online the coded structure diagrams of more than 3.8 million chemical substances.

Searching by Generic Groups

Hard-copy abstract journal section divisions may be used as search entries where they are made available on the tape. For instance, in the Chemical Condensates file it is possible to formulate the strategy so that it requests the computer to search a certain aspect only in relation to a given subject. Such a concept as the mathematical group theory might be of interest in relation to polymers and plastics, or in relation to nuclear chemistry. For the first area of interest, the strategy would request, on the Chemical Condensates file, all items with the keyword GROUP THEORY that appear in sections 035 through 046. For the second area of interest, the strategy would request all items with the keyword GROUP THEORY which appear in sections 075 or 076.

The Chemical Abstracts section number is often of use in restricting a search. In Fig. 3.7 the section is 029, Organometallic and Organometalloidal Compounds. If the interest is in the nuclear magnetic resonance

Entry Points   51

(NMR) of organometallic compounds, the best way to search would be to link the term NMR and the section number, since, as in Fig. 3.7, the name of the organometallic compound but not the term "organometallic" will usually appear among the index terms.

Other files may have divisions identified by alphabetic titles, as shown in Fig. 3.13 for the Engineering Index file. Such potential linkages are usually covered by the normal listing of alphanumeric terms of interest, but the generic headings of the file, where these are in the search base, are additional entry points that should not be overlooked.

Another example of the use of generic headings is the use of Standard Industrial Classifications (SIC) codes in patent and business files such as the Predicasts files.

```
CORROSION
    (Use for general subject of corrosion of materials
    applying code 539 for metals corrosion, code 631
    for cavitation corrosion, code 802 for chemical
    corrosion. Otherwise use the subheading -Corrosion
    under the heading for the thing being corroded,
    and cross-reference to CORROSION. See also
    CORROSION PROTECTION)
    Cavitation Origin   See CAVITATION CORROSION
    Electrochemical
    Electrolytic
    Fretting
    High Temperature Effects
    Inhibitors   See CORROSION PROTECTION -Inhibitors
    Metal   See METALS AND ALLOYS -Corrosion
    Pitting
    Seawater
    Stress Corrosion Cracking
    Tropics
    Underground
CORROSION PROTECTION
    (Use for general subject and for applications not
    elsewhere classifiable. Otherwise use the subheading
    -Corrosion Protection under the heading for the thing
    being protected against corrosion, and cross-reference
    to CORROSION PROTECTION)
    Anodic   see CORROSION PROTECTION, ANODIC
    Cathodic   See CORROSION PROTECTION, CATHODIC
    Inhibitors
CORROSION PROTECTION, ANODIC
    (Use for general subject and for applications not
    elsewhere classifiable. Otherwise use subheading
    -Anodic Protection under heading for thing so
    protected, and cross-reference to CORROSION
    PROTECTION, ANODIC)
CORROSION PROTECTION, CATHODIC
    (Use for general subject and for applications not
    elsewhere classifiable. Otherwise use subheading
    -Cathodic Protection under heading for thing so
    protected, and cross-reference to CORROSION
    PROTECTION, CATHODIC)
```

Figure 3.13   Example of subject headings and subheadings from SHE [33]. Reproduced with permission by Engineering Index, Inc.

Ranked by Accession No.

EI 740702483	NOISE - AN INDUSTRIAL POLLUTANT OF INTERNATIONAL CONCERN.	CPALAQ	1973
EI 740700815	NOISE ABATEMENT IN SHEET METAL WORKING PRACTICE.	DFBOAF	Feb 1974
EI 740700814	NOISE REDUCTION IN INDUSTRIAL PRACTICE.	DFBOAF	Feb 1974
EI 740604369	CURBING NOISE WITH PARTIAL ENCLOSURES.	MADEAP	Apr 1974
EI 740603888	POSSIBILITIES AND RANGE OF APPLICATION OF THE SILENT CONSTRUCTION METHODS FOR URBAN CONSTRUCTION ENGINEERING.	BMBTAN	Mar 1974

Ranked by Publication Date

EI 740604369	CURBING NOISE WITH PARTIAL ENCLOSURES.	MADEAP	Apr 1974
EI 740603888	POSSIBILITIES AND RANGE OF APPLICATION OF THE SILENT CONSTRUCTION METHODS FOR URBAN CONSTRUCTION ENGINEERING.	BMBTAN	Mar 1974
EI 740700814	NOISE REDUCTION IN INDUSTRIAL PRACTICE.	DFBOAF	Feb 1974
EI 740700815	NOISE ABATEMENT IN SHEET METAL WORKING PRACTICE.	DFBOAF	Feb 1974
EI 740702483	NOISE - AN INDUSTRIAL POLLUTANT OF INTERNATIONAL CONCERN.	CPALAQ	1973

Figure 3.14 Comparison of ranking by accession number and ranking by publication date.

Limiting the Search by Publication Date

A search can be limited to within a certain time period. A request can be made for output of files more recent than a certain date, or only between two dates. Usually such a limitation is based on accession numbers corresponding to file accession dates, the request being for output between two accession numbers. By specifying a journal publication date, where the field bearing that date is a searchable entity, a different chronological listing can be obtained, as shown in Fig. 3.14.

SEARCHING BY BOOLEAN LOGIC

Although there are several methods of relating the terms selected to apply to a search, the most successful method has been the use of Boolean logic [17,18,19,20,21]. Most search programs for bibliographic files are now based on Boolean logic. Other methods which have been used employ weighted terms [22], or codes such as "links and roles" [23] to indicate the relationship between selected terms.

The Boolean logic search method makes use of the logic operators OR, AND, and NOT.

Searching by Boolean Logic   53

The Logical Sum

The OR operator indicates that any of the terms linked with the OR connector may give a match or hit. If the terms are supplied as

    SOUND + NOISE + ACOUSTIC

where + is the equivalent of OR, the search will retrieve any item in which one or more of those terms occurs as a searchable surrogate. The ORed terms are frequently synonyms, since they are selected as terms which may be expected to pull documents on the subject of interest. They need not be synonymous, however. The terms INSULATION and SOUND LEVEL METERS are not synonyms and yet they could be ORed to identify documents on the subject of noise reduction.

The Logical Product

A logical product of terms is a series of terms connected by AND. The operator AND signifies that all the terms linked by AND must be among the document surrogates in order for the document to be pulled. For example,

    SOUND * SUPPRESSION * INDUSTRY

where * is the equivalent of AND, is a group of terms that may be expected to find documents related to the suppression of sound in industrial surroundings. Since the operator AND requires the presence of all surrogates connected by AND in order to make a match, in the above logical product all three terms—SOUND and SUPPRESSION and INDUSTRY—must be present for a hit. The search program may be written so that greater efficiency in searching occurs if the term with the fewest postings appears first in the logical product, the one with the next fewest postings second, and so on; because only items in which the first term is present will be examined for the second term, and so forth. A logical product may also be referred to as an "intersection," because it represents a group of items formed by the intersection of items identified by one term with another group of items which can be identified by the second term. This concept arose from the use of Venn diagrams to clarify explanations of Boolean logic [20].

Negative Logic

If the terms are written as

    INSULATING - HEAT

where - is the equivalent of NOT, the search will retrieve any item for which INSULATING appears as a searchable surrogate, <u>unless</u> HEAT also appears among the surrogates. Negative logic, a request to list all documents except those in which a certain term is present, is a necessary tool for effective mechanical searching. It can be used as part of a logical sum. For instance, a request to list all documents which have any of the terms

BLUE + GREEN + VIOLET - RED

will yield all documents in which BLUE, GREEN, or VIOLET is present, except those in which RED is also present.

Negative logic can also be used to modify a logical product. For example, the

(GARDENS * BULBS) - LIGHT BULBS

will give all items satisfying the intersection unless the term LIGHT BULBS is present.

One quality of negative logic that should always be considered is the override function. In the above examples, the presence of the negated term eliminates the whole document, parts of which might have been of interest. Strategies can be manipulated so that the negative does not apply to the whole strategy. An example of such a strategy would be

((MOUNTAINS + WILDERNESS) * (HIKING + BACKPACKING)) +

(MOUNTAIN RECREATION - SKIING)

Here the interest is in hiking, backpacking, and related recreation in mountains and wilderness areas. An index term MOUNTAIN RECREATION is identified for the file, but negative logic is used to eliminate skiing, which is not of interest to the searcher.

Nested Parentheses

The term "nested parentheses" refers to the capability of indicating the performance of logical operations on a number of terms and using the result as a term in another logical operation. An example of such an operation is the following strategy:

(LABRADOR + RETRIEVER + ((HUNTING + BIRD) * DOG)) *

(TRAIN + TEACH)

This strategy is designed to request items about the training of dogs, but restricting the dogs to only hunting dogs. Note that each left-hand parenthesis must be balanced by a right-hand parenthesis for the program to function. Some programs will not permit the submission of nested parentheses to this depth. No real problem is created by the rejection of nested parentheses in depth by an online program, since the operations may be performed in series. An example of such a series follows. As each search word is entered, the program gives the stored set of items an identifying number.

Searching by Boolean Logic

1 LABRADOR
2 RETRIEVER
3 HUNTING
4 BIRD
5 DOG
6 TRAIN
7 TEACH

The terms are combined by means of the identifying numbers into sets. The sets are combined to produce the final statement (set 9 below), which is the basis for a request for printed-out results.

8 (3 + 4) * 5
9 (1 + 2 + 8) * (6 + 7)

The Three-Aspect Approach

Most searches of mechanical files use the logical product of logical sums. Logical sums are used because synonyms must always be considered, as must the different points of view from which different authors may approach a problem. Were it possible to search the complete text of documents, it would be feasible for a search to employ only phrases that expressed exactly the area of interest. But since for most files the approach is from index terms, of which there may be from 3 to 20 per document, the most useful way to pattern the search is to use several sets or groups of terms because, unless the indexing is a small closed set (or limited listing), there will always be a wide variety of descriptive terms for similar documents. When the terms are well chosen, three sets can be expected to yield a definitive answer. Sometimes it seems as though there should be four or five sets to be truly precise, but such precision is not attainable based on the limited and inaccurate indexing at our disposal. With four sets, and most often even with only three, there will be a result of no hits, because among the identifying terms representing relevant items, terms from one or more of the applicable sets will be missing.

As an example of the difficulties inherent in searching term combinations, the following simple strategy is given. The interest was in government regulations of noise on construction sites. From a previously run search of the Engineering Index file, four relevant documents were selected. The indexing for these documents was:

1. CONSTRUCTION EQUIPMENT; NOISE ABATEMENT; LEGISLATION
2. INDUSTRIAL PLANTS; NOISE ABATEMENT; NOISE, ACOUSTIC
3. INDUSTRIAL PLANTS; NOISE ABATEMENT; LEGISLATION; OSHA REGULATIONS
4. NOISE ABATEMENT; LEGISLATION

A search using only one term, NOISE ABATEMENT, would have found all four relevant documents, but only about 5% of the total output retrieved on the COMPENDEX file would have been relevant to the user's interest. If two terms, NOISE ABATEMENT and LEGISLATION, were required for a hit, three of the four relevant documents listed above would have been found. If three terms, CONSTRUCTION EQUIPMENT, NOISE ABATEMENT, and LEGISLATION, were ANDed, only one of the four documents would have been found. If the term INDUSTRIAL PLANTS was ORed to the CONSTRUCTION EQUIPMENT term, two of the four documents would have been found—an improvement—although many documents about INDUSTRIAL PLANTS would not be relevant. The more precise three-way strategy

NOISE ABATEMENT * LEGISLATION * (CONSTRUCTION EQUIPMENT + INDUSTRIAL PLANTS)

still does not improve the results from the two-way

NOISE ABATEMENT * LEGISLATION

The Logical Product of Three Logical Sums   When preparing a search, the three-aspect approach, which may zero in on pertinent documents, is a good first approach. For example, consider a search for possible solutions to the problem of noise in a pipe manufacturing plant. There are a number of noise-related words such as NOISE, SOUND, and ACOUSTICS. There are also words related to suppressing sound, such as ABATEMENT, SUPPRESSION, INSULATION, INSULATING, CONTROL, ELIMINATION, REDUCTION, SILENCERS, MUFFLERS, and FILTERS. Next there are words related to the environment in which the noise is to be suppressed, such as INDUSTRY, INDUSTRIAL, PIPE PLANT, and TUBE MILL. Consideration of methods from other environments which might be applicable would add to the environmental terms the terms FOUNDRY, FACTORY, and STEEL MILLS. A strategy set up on the basis of these expanded concepts might be

(NOISE + SOUND + ACOUSTICS) * (ABATEMENT + SUPPRESSION + INSULATION + INSULATING + CONTROL + ELIMINATION + REDUCTION + SILENCERS + MUFFLERS + FILTERS) * (INDUSTRY + INDUSTRIAL + PIPE PLANT + TUBE MILL + FOUNDRY + FACTORY + STEEL MILL)

This postulated strategy asks the computer to list all items which have among their identifying terms at least one of the first group of ORed terms, and at least one from the second group, and at least one from the third group. At least three terms are required to cause a hit. The following results demonstrate the efficiency of such a strategy:

Group A: The following relevant documents will be found if the file is searched by title alone:

1. "Noise Reduction in Industrial Halls Obtained by Acoustical Treatment of Ceilings and Walls."
2. "Feasible Engineering Noise Control for the Primary Metals Industry."
3. "Possibilities of and Problems Involved in Industrial Noise Abatement."

Group B: The following additional relevant documents will be found if the file is searched by title and index terms:

4. "Curbing Noise with Partial Enclosures." Descriptors: INDUSTRIAL PLANTS, NOISE ABATEMENT.
5. "Engineering Approaches to Plant Noise Control." Descriptors: INDUSTRIAL PLANTS, NOISE ABATEMENT, ACOUSTICS, MACHINERY.
6. "Environment Inside the Forges Can Be Improved." Descriptors: FORGING, NOISE ABATEMENT, INDUSTRIAL ENGINEERING.

Group C: The following relevant documents in the file will not hit, because only two of the requested lists of terms is matched.

7. "Reduction of Machinery Noise." Descriptors: NOISE ABATEMENT, HEARING DAMAGE, SOUND PROPRGATION, MACHINES.
8. "Barriers for Noise Control." Descriptors: NOISE, NOISE ABATEMENT, MACHINERY.
9. "Stop Plant Noise . . . At the Source or Along the Way." Descriptors: NOISE PROBLEMS, INDUSTRIAL PLANTS, SOUND.

On the basis of these results a new, more effective strategy could be written. It should be emphasized that the addition of enough terms to identify all the relevant documents will increase nonrelevant retrievals.

<u>The Relaxed Three-Aspect Approach</u> In searches in which the number of hits resulting from a three-way intersection is smaller than expected, the three-aspect approach can be relaxed by using two-way intersections. If the aspects are represented as follows:

A * B * C

the relaxed strategy would be

((A + B) * C) + (A * B)

An example of the design of such a strategy is as follows. The topic of interest is methods of detecting beneficial effects of surface treatment of low carbon steels. Three aspects were selected and, with the help of thesauri and reference books [4, 24—29] a number of usable terms were listed:

A	B	C
CARBON STEELS	NITRIDING SURFACE FINISHING ELECTROCHEMICAL MACHINING PROTECTIVE COATINGS WEAR INHIBITORS SURFACE REACTIONS	ACOUSTIC MEASUREMENTS NONDESTRUCTIVE TESTS FRACTOGRAPHY SURFACE CRACKS FATIGUE TESTS PENETRANTS ELECTRON MICROSCOPES MICROSTRUCTURE SERVICE LIFE WEAR TESTS X-RAY ANALYSIS

Using the formula for a relaxed strategy

$$((A + B) * C) + (A * B)$$

a search was made of a file which is searchable only by index terms, and a list of documents was printed out. The following five documents, identified only by number and document index terms, are examples of relevant documents:

1. HIGH STRENGTH STEELS, WEAR TESTS, MECHANICAL PROPERTIES, SURFACE REACTIONS
2. NITRIDING, TECHNOLOGY ASSESSMENT, CARBON STEELS, SURFACE FINISHING
3. ACOUSTIC MEASUREMENTS, FRACTOGRAPHY, CARBON STEELS, FATIGUE TESTS, PENETRANTS
4. ELECTROCHEMICAL MACHINING, METAL SURFACES, CARBON STEELS
5. BORIDES, CARBON STEELS, FRICTION MEASUREMENT, PROTECTIVE COATINGS, WEAR INHIBITORS, ELECTRON MICROSCOPES, MICROSTRUCTURE, SERVICE LIFE, SURFACE STABILITY, WEAR TESTS, X-RAY ANALYSIS

Examination of the results of possible strategies using the three selected aspect lists of terms gives the following figures for the above five documents.

Weighting 59

Strategy	Number of documents found
A * B * C	1
A * (B + C)	4
B * (A + C)	4
C * (A + B)	4
A * B	3
A * C	2
B * C	3
(A * (B + C)) + (B * C)	5

A strategy of the form A * (B + C) rather than the complete relaxed strategy if often used when it is felt that one aspect, such as CARBON STEELS, is necessary for relevance. In this case, if the analyst had added HIGH STRENGTH STEELS to the list of A terms, the strategy A * (B + C) would have been adequate, at least for the five documents represented. While all high strength steels are not low carbon steels, the term HIGH STRENGTH STEEL is applicable to low carbon steels.

WEIGHTING

Weighting is another approach besides Boolean logic to the relationship between terms. A relative numerical weight is assigned to each of the search terms and represents the importance of each term in the strategy. A hit occurs when the sum of the numerical weights of the index terms of a document achieves a predetermined threshold weight. For example, in a search on the subject of the marine corrosion of stainless or specialty steels, weights might be assigned as follows:

Term	Weight
STAINLESS	50
SPECIALTY	50
CHROMIUM	20
NICKEL	20
STEEL	30
CORROSION	40
SEAWATER	50
MARINE	50
Threshold weight for retrieval of item	100

For the above strategy, items having the following index terms would give hits:

1. STAINLESS, STEEL, CORROSION, SEAWATER   170
2. CHROMIUM, NICKEL, STEEL, CORROSION   110
3. NICKEL, CORROSION, SEAWATER, MARINE, ALLOY   160

Item 1 is the kind of item the analyst wanted; item 2 may be relevant, and item 3 is probably not relevant. Because the Boolean logic method specifies relationships between terms, it is much less apt to give unpredictable results in the hands of the amateur than is the weighted strategy.

Using Weights to Negate

Weighted strategies operate better for negation than does Boolean negative logic, because in weighting the negative (minus numerical value) can be overridden by a large positive sum. For instance, for the above steel corrosion search a negative nickel alloy term could have been added to the strategy to prevent hits on items about nickel alloys but not about steels. Item 3 would have been cancelled if NICKEL ALLOY had been among the surrogates and if NICKEL ALLOY -70 had been in the strategy. If NICKEL ALLOY had been among the surrogates of item 1, the item would still have been retrieved because it was about stainless steel as well as nickel alloy.

Using Weights to Sort

Weighting can also be used as a sorting technique. Items with the greatest weight are listed first, and other items in descending order by weight. When using weights to sort, weights may be assigned only to significant terms, with the others operating on zero weight. When weighting is combined with Boolean logic, a useful listing can be obtained in which items that correspond exactly to the specific interest are listed first.

Weighted strategies have been used with great skill by those trained in their use, notably at Aerospace Research Applications Center (ARC) of Indiana University and, in combination with Boolean logic, at the University of Georgia [30].

THE USE OF POSTINGS IN STRATEGY BUILDING

Ascertaining the number of documents in the file for a given term or group of terms is of considerable value in preparing a strategy.

The Use of Postings in Strategy Building 61

Suppose a postings dictionary gives the following figures:

CORROSION	1428
SEAWATER	942
SHIPS	456
FOULING ORGANISMS	9
STEEL	5920

A strategy might be set up as:

((SHIPS + STEEL) * SEAWATER * CORROSION) + FOULING ORGANISMS

If the strategy was submitted online, the following postings could be ascertained:

CORROSION * STEEL	1132
SEAWATER * STEEL	598
SEAWATER * CORROSION * STEEL	321
SHIPS * SEAWATER * CORROSION	3
SHIPS * CORROSION	197

It seems probable, since SHIPS usually implies the presence of SEAWATER, that the hits resulting from SHIPS * CORROSION would mostly relate to the corrosion of steel by seawater. The wisest strategy then appears to be

(SEAWATER * CORROSION * STEEL) + (SHIPS * CORROSION) + FOULING ORGANISMS

Because the number of postings to FOULING ORGANISMS is so small, it seems best to search that term unmodified rather than to risk losing a pertinent document because the right index term was not paired with FOULING ORGANISMS. The corrosion of "ships" implies the presence of seawater. The probability of missing relevant documents if the term SEAWATER is required is shown by comparing the numbers 197 and 3. The result 321 for the three-way intersection SEAWATER * CORROSION * STEEL is a good yield. SEAWATER * STEEL would yield additional relevant documents, but also many documents that are not relevant. Another approach would be to search SEAWATER * STEEL, but to limit either how far back in time the search should go, or how many documents should be chosen—say the most recent 100 or 200. The analyst must make such decisions from a knowledge of whether the most valuable documents would be recent or not recent. Obviously, CORROSION * STEEL would yield many documents not concerned with seawater corrosion.

EFFECT OF RECALL AND PRECISION ON STRATEGY BUILDING

The critical part of strategy building is to so balance "precision" (the percentage of retrieved items which are relevant) and "recall" (the percentage of relevant file items which are retrieved) that a good listing of relevant references is achieved, with few misses of relevant references, and a small number of nonrelevant items. The latter are often referred to as "false drops," a carry-over in nomenclature from the early days of sorting notched cards. The two measures of search efficiency, precision and recall, are discussed in more detail in Chap. 5.

High recall and high precision are not hard to attain for a general inquiry. For a very specific inquiry, a broad strategy may achieve fairly high recall but low precision. On the other hand, for a specific inquiry there may be a specific term which will result in low recall but high precision. Writing a strategy broad enough to net all the relevant items in the file (100% recall) will result in low precision for the average request. Writing a tight strategy with high precision (90-100%) usually means that a large number of relevant items will be missed.

Discipline Tailored Files

For special purposes, if the questions addressed to the system were precisely coded and known in advance, a precisely coded system could be set up that would yield both high precision and high recall. The usual technical file, oriented to subject terms rather than to data is, however, designed to accept inquiries directed to many combinations of concepts.

It is difficult to predict the nature of future inquiries because the future directions of scientific interests are not known. At present the fields of energy and environmental control are obviously of growing interest, and new files are being built oriented to those interests. Discipline-oriented files can give quite good precision and recall values because one aspect of the question, such as "energy" or "environment," has been already applied to the items on the file.

Automatic Strategy Preparation

With the growing use of online searching, it can be predicted that future mechanical searching will be tailored for the user's use of online files. Automatic strategy preparation can be programmed, hingeing on the user's selection of relevant items from displays at the terminal. Automatic profile preparation is discussed in [31] and [32]. At present a profile can be set up by study of online displays, but the cost is prohibitive. Built-in programming to produce the profile from items selected by the user would be costly. Such costs will no doubt be reduced by future improvements in mechanical information retrieval.

Appendix I

SUMMARY

The strategy of presenting search terms to the computer to obtain a printout of references relevant to a request results from consideration of the way the search program operates. Most such programs today are based on Boolean logic, including the logical sum, the logical product, negative logic, and combinations of these capabilities. The available entry points—such as subject words or terms, authors, journal identifications, numerical data, and chemical structure—must be known. The number of items in the file per term (postings) are helpful in setting up the strategy. Weighting of terms, with or without Boolean logic, is a capability of some programs. Factors affecting the recall and precision of the search must be considered.

An example of a technical search is given in Appendix II.

APPENDIX I Searching Work Flow

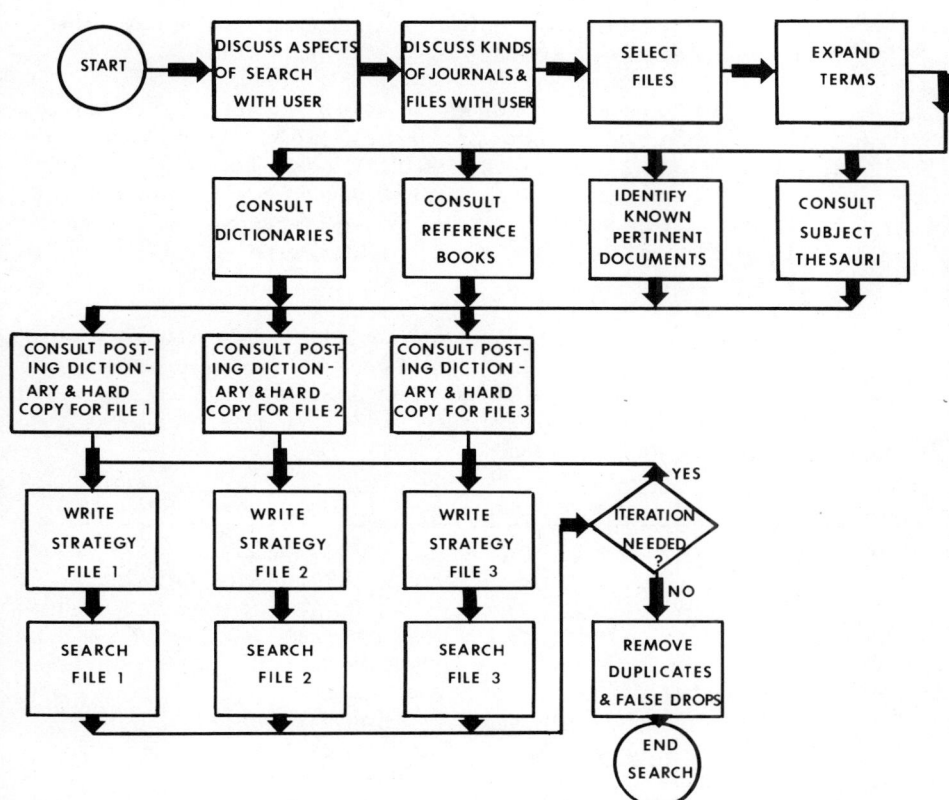

APPENDIX II   Example of Search Procedures and Results

An example of search procedures and results is presented in this appendix.
   An industrial client requested information on the general subject "welding of stainless steel." After consultation between the company user and the analyst, the following written statement of the interest was prepared. "Thin-gauge stainless steel sheet, 0.031 inches to 0.125 inches thick, is welded to make a special form. The stainless steel is of the 300 series, usually 304 (18-8), or 316 (18-8-Mo). Problems such as weld distortion, and crevices at the weld in which corrosion and pitting take place, have been encountered. The welding techniques used are TIG, MIG, stick, and HELIARC. The final finish is of primary importance. The weld seam should be smooth, attractive, leak-free, and corrosion-resistant."
   From this statement it seemed advisable to search for welding of thin-gauge stainless steel, not limiting the search by weld technique. While the client was primarily interested in improving the results of the welding techniques suggested, any information indicating that the desired results might be obtained by another technique should certainly be brought to his attention.
   Three files out of the many available were chosen as being most likely to provide the information desired:

1. METADEX, because, while small, it is a disciplinary file directed toward all aspects of alloy preparation, processing, and properties
2. ENGINEERING INDEX (COMPENDEX), because it is oriented to all aspects of engineering including techniques for metal forming
3. NASA, because this file contains well-prepared coverage of the properties and forming of metallic alloys, especially as related to space research

Using the three-aspect approach, the chosen file entry groups were stainless steel, welding, and corrosion and defects. For these three aspects, using the conversations with the client, thesauri [4, 25, 26], hard-copy indexes of the three chosen files [27, 28, 29], and reference books [24], the following terms were selected:

A. Stainless steel	B. Welding	C. Corrosion and defects
STAINLESS STEEL	WELDING	CORROSION
	WELDS	CORROSION RESISTANCE
AISI 304	WELDABLE	INTERGRANULAR CORROSION
AISI 308	WELDED	FERRITE
AISI 316	WELD	DELTA
AUSTENITIC STEEL	WELDABILITY	SIGMA
	JOINING	DUCTILITY
	JOINTS	QUALITY
		POROSITY
		WELD DEFECTS

Appendix II

Study of the third aspect, corrosion and defects, indicated that many types of weld defects may be discussed in documents of potential interest. The weld defects may result from the formation of second phases ferrite, delta, or sigma. General terms like "quality" may be used. It was decided to search on the straight two-way intersection of stainless steel terms and welding terms. The following strategy was prepared:

(STAINLESS + AUSTENITIC + 304 + 308 + 316) * (WELD/ + JOIN/)

where / indicates trunication. It was believed that the result of this strategy would be an overall picture of the subject of welding of stainless steel, to which the aspect "thin gauge" could be applied by judicious weeding by the analyst. An example file of retrieved documents (five from each file) is listed by title below:

From Metadex:

1. "Backup Tape Boosts Weld Quality and Saves"
2. "Process for the Production of Butt Welds for Pressure Vessels"
3. "Production of a Thin Austenitic Steel Plate Lining for a Plastic-Metal Vessel"
4. "Gas-Tungsten-Arc Hot-Wire Welding—A Versatile New Production Tool"
5. "MIG-Welding of Thin Sheets"

From Engineering Index:

6. "Role of Ferrite in Stainless Steel Welds"
7. "Progress Toward a more Weldable A-286 M-1."
8. "Making Sense out of Ferrite Requirements in Welding Stainless Steels"
9. "Creep Rupture Properties of Welded Joints of Type AISI 304 and 316 Austenitic Stainless Steels"
10. "Formation of Sigma Phase in 26 Cr:6 Ni Stainless Steel"

From NASA:

11. "Ferrite in Austenitic Stainless Steel Weld Metal"
12. "Mechanical Behavior and Weldability of a High Chromium Ferrite Stainless Steel as a Function of Purity"
13. "Mechanical Properties and Weldability of Nitrogen-Bearing Austenitic Steels"
14. "Relation Between Mechanical Properties and Microstructure in CRE Type 308 Weldments"
15. Creep Properties of a Type 308 Stainless Steel Pressure Vessel Weld With Controlled Residual Elements"

All of the above sample documents were the result of the two-way strategy given above. If all three of the aspects had been united in a three-way strategy, all of the sample documents from the NASA file would have hit, but only three out of five for both Metadex and Engineering Index. This is only a general indication of the results of searching by loose and tight strategies. The total number retrieved items from all of the files was 473, of which 142 were judged to be relevant.

The precision for the "loose" strategy was therefore 30%. With the "tight" strategy it would have been much closer to 100%. When a search precision approaches 80% or above, doubts should be entertained as to whether all relevant items have been discovered.

REFERENCES

1. Jerry R. Byrne. "Relative Effectiveness of Titles, Abstracts, and Subject Headings for Machine Retrieval from the Compendex Services." J. Amer. Soc. Inf. Sci. 26(4), July-August 1975, 223.
2. David L. Dayton. "New Aids for Formulating Searches of CAS Indexes and Computer-Readable Files." CAS Rep. August 1975, p. 3.
3. National Technical Information Service. Medical Subject Headings (MESH). Department of Commerce, Springfield, Virginia, 1974.
4. National Aeronautics and Space Administration. NASA Thesaurus. NASA-SP-7050, Washington, D.C., 1967.
5. Lockheed Information Systems. "A Brief Guide to DIALOG Searching." Palo Alto, California, September 1976.
6. Users Manual for Interactive PIRETS, 2nd edition. The University of Pittsburgh, University of Pittsburgh Staff. Pittsburgh, Pennsylvania, November 1, 1976.
7. Donald T. Hawkins. "Unconventional Uses of Online Information Retrieval Systems." J. Amer. Soc. Inf. Sci. 28(1), January 1977, 13.
8. Donald B. Cleveland. "An N-dimensional Retrieval Model." J. Amer. Soc. Inf. Sci. 27(5/6), September-October 1976, 342.
9. Ellis Mount. "A National Standard for Bibliographic References." J. Amer. Soc. Inf. Sci. 28(1), January 1977, 3.
10. BioSciences Information Service of Biological Abstracts, Chemical Abstracts Service, and Engineering Index, Inc. Bibliographic Guide for Editors and Authors. The American Chemical Society, Washington, D.C., 1974.
11. H. R. Schenk and F. Wegmuller. "Substructure Search by Means of the Chemical Abstracts Service Chemical Registry II System." J. Chem. Inf. Comput. Sci. 16(3), 1976, 153.
12. E. G. Smith. The Wiswesser Line-Formula Chemical Notation. McGraw-Hill, New York, 1968.
13. Chemical Abstract Services. Chemical Titles. Amer. Chem. Soc., Washington, D.C.

References

14. M. L. Huber. "Chemical Structure Codes in Perspective." J. Chem. Doc. 5(4), 1965, 4.
15. E. Garfield, C. E. Granito, and A. E. Petrarca. "Information Retrieval Services and Methods." In Encyclopedia of Chemical Technology, R. E. Kirk and D. F. Othmer, eds, supplement volume, 2nd edition. Wiley, New York, 1971, p. 510.
16. Nick A. Farmer, Carole A. Schermer, and Ronald L. Wigington. "The American Chemical Society Composition System." CAS Rep. 5, October 1976, p. 3.
17. George Boole. The Mathematical Analysis of Logic. Cambridge, 1847.
18. Allen Kent. Textbook on Mechanized Information Retrieval. Wiley, Interscience, New York, 1962.
19. Joseph Becker and R. M. Hayes. Information Storage and Retrieval. Wiley, New York, 1963.
20. F. W. Lancaster and E. G. Fayen. Information Retrieval On-Line. Melville Publishing, Wiley, 1973.
21. Jack Minker, Eero Peltola, and Gerald A. Wilson. "Document Retrieval Experiments Using Cluster Analysis." J. Amer. Soc. Inf. Sci. 24(4), 1973, 246.
22. H. G. Sommar and D. E. Dennis. "A New Method of Weighted Term Searching with a Highly Structured Thesaurus." Proc. ASIS 6, 1969, 193.
23. F. W. Lancaster. Information Retrieval Systems. Wiley, New York, 1968.
24. American Society for Metals. Metals Handbook. Metals Park, Ohio, 8th edition, 1961-1978.
25. American Society for Metals. ASM Thesaurus of Metallurgical Terms. Metals Park, Ohio.
26. Engineers Joint Council. DOD/EJC Thesaurus of Engineering Terms. New York, 1967.
27. American Society for Metals and the Institute of Metals. Metals Abstracts and Metals Abstracts Index. Metals Park, Ohio.
28. Engineering Index, Inc. Engineering Index. New York, New York.
29. National Aeronautics and Space Administration. Scientific and Technical Aerospace Reports. Washington, D. C.
30. Margaret K. Park. "Computer Based Bibliographic Retrieval Service: The View from the Center." Spec. Lib. 64(4), 1973, 187.
31. Alan Robson and Janet S. Longman. "Automatic Aids to Profile Construction." J. Amer. Soc. Inf. Sci. 27(4), July-August, 1976, 213.
32. John M. Carroll and Jean M. Tague. "Use of an Automatic Text Analyzer in Preparation of SDI Profiles." J. Amer. Soc. Inf. Sci. 24(4), July-August 1973, 277.
33. Engineering Index, Inc. Engineering Index Thesaurus. CCM Information Corporation, New York, 1972.

chapter 4
Presentation of Search Results

INTRODUCTION

The goal of literature searching is useful information presented so that it can be easily applied. One fact noted in a pocket notebook may be an intellectual triumph; twenty or thirty pages of unorganized notes, no matter how valuable to the notetaker, are not useful to someone else.

Computer printout from a mechanized literature search may consist simply of bibliographic citations sequenced chronologically by date of insertion into the searchable file. With different print instruction programs, however, the citations may appear in reverse order by date of publication (the latest first), or grouped by country of origin, or grouped by operative index terms. All of these, no matter what the print order, are raw computer output in which false drops may occur. It does not take an unreasonable length of time to select three or four documents which are potentially interesting from two pages of a computer printout of bibliographic citations. A stack of computer sheets one or two inches high, however, may require three or four hours of reading time in order to make a choice of documents to be read entirely. Both the two-page printout and the stack of printout may be the result of a well-tailored search, differing only in the breadth of the subject or the frequency with which publication appears on the subject.

The successful information broker, counselor, consultant, or liaison person will edit the results of the search as far as he is able. The edited results of a literature search can be presented as a bibliography, a bibliography with abstracts, a bibliography with notes, a structured bibliography, a digest or review of source articles, or a summary report of the results of the literature search.

PRODUCTS OF MECHANIZED RETRIEVAL

Printouts, Tapes

The usual output of an automated information retrieval system is computer sheets containing in a specified order (usually chronological with the latest first) a list of bibliographic citations, with or without abstracts. Each bibliographic citation consists of authors; title; journal name, volume, year, and page; identifying descriptors or index terms; language; and authors' affiliations. The same information can be recorded on magnetic or paper tape. Figure 4.1 is an example of a bibliographic printout. The items on the printout can also be printed on IBM or file cards, each item on a separate card.

```
type26/5/1-3
26/5/1
GA397000730    0487222
  Comparison   of   two   background   correction   procedures   for   X-ray
fluorescence trace element analysis of some standard samples
  WYROBISCH. W
  Geostand Newsl (Paris)    1/2 P107-109   1977   JRNL CODE: GNEWPI
  LANGUAGE: ENGLISH
  DESCRIPTORS:    GEOCHEMICAL    TECHNIQUES:    LABORATORY    METHODS:
GEOMATHEMATICS: GEOCHEMICAL STANDARDS
  DESCRIPTOR CODES: 663000" 820000: 690000: 660500

26/5/2
GA397000726    0487218
  The state  of  art   trace element analysis of geological samples as
derived from results on standard rock samples
  RUBESKA, I
  Geostand Newsl (Paris)    1/1 P15-20   1977 JRNL CODE:GNEWPI
  LANGUAGE: ENGLISH

  DESCRIPTORS: GEOCHEMICAL TECHNIQUES; LABORATORY METHODS; GEOCHEMICAL
STANDARDS
  DESCRIPTOR CODES:    663000; 820000; 660500

26/5/3
GA397000181    0486674
  Sulphur isotope and trace metal composition  of stratiform sulphides
as an ore guide in the Canadian Shield
  SECCOMBE,  PK
  CONF. DATES: 16 AUGUST TO 25 AUGUST NO: 76-0160
  J. Geochem Explor (Amsterdam)   8/1-2 P117-137    1977    JRNL CODE:
JGEXPI
  LANGUAGE: ENGLISH
  DESCRIPTORS:  BEDROCK ANALYSIS;  EXPLORATION FOR METALS;   STRATIFORM
DEPOSITS; COPPER ORES; ZINC ORES; ISOTOPE GEOCHEMISTRY
  AUXILIARY DESCRIPTORS: CANADIAN SHIELD
  DESCRIPTOR CODES:  336700; 333400; 420300; 425000; 427000; 670000
  AUXILIARY DESCRIPTOR CODES: 711000
```

Figure 4.1 Printout from an online run on Lockheed's GEOARCHIVE file. Reproduced with permission from Lockheed Missiles & Space Company, Inc.

Indexes

Different programming can produce a keyword in context (KWIC) index (Fig. 4.2), a keyword out of context (KWOC) index (Fig. 4.3), as well as a straight alphabetic index based on the descriptors in the file (Fig. 4.4). It is possible also to produce a more generic index by use of a series of search strategies, the results of which are listed under appropriate generic terms (Fig. 4.5). All of these products require a reference list or journal from which the full citation of the items identified (by number) can be read. A description of mechanized methods of producing the <u>Chemical Abstracts</u> volume indexes is given in [1].

scence trace element	1	<u>analysis</u> of some standard samples.
of art trace element	2	<u>analysis</u> of geological samples as
amples. The state of	2	<u>art</u> trace element analysis of geo-
s. Comparison of two	1	<u>background</u> correction procedures f
an ore guide in the	3	<u>Canadian</u> Shield. Sulphur isotope a
ome standard samples.	1	<u>Comparison</u> of two background corr-
tope and trace metal	3	<u>composition</u> of stratiform sulphide
on of two background	1	<u>correction</u> procedures for X-ray fl
eological samples as	2	<u>derived</u> from results on standard r
y fluorescence trace	1	<u>element</u> analysis of some standard
e state of art trace	2	<u>element</u> analysis of geological sam
procedures for X-ray	1	<u>fluorescence</u> trace element analysi
element analysis of	2	<u>geological</u> samples as derived from
sulphides as an ore	3	<u>guide</u> in the Canadian Shield. Sulp
dian Shield. Sulphur	3	<u>isotope</u> and trace metal compositio
ur isotope and trace	3	<u>metal</u> composition of stratiform su
form sulphides as an	3	<u>ore</u> guide in the Canadian Shield.
ackground correction	1	<u>procedures</u> for X-ray fluorescence
ples as derived from	2	<u>results</u> on standard rock samples.
results on standard	2	<u>rock</u> samples. The state of art tr
sis of some standard	1	<u>samples.</u> Comparison of two backgr
lts on standard rock	2	<u>samples.</u> The state of art trace e
uide in the Canadian	3	<u>Shield.</u> Sulphur isotope and trace
ent analysis of some	1	<u>standard</u> samples. Comparison of t
ived from results on	2	<u>standard</u> rock samples. The state
rd rock samples. The	2	<u>state</u> of art trace element analysi
metal composition of	3	<u>stratiform</u> sulphides as an ore gui
sition of stratiform	3	<u>sulphides</u> as an ore guide in the c
the Canadian Shield.	3	<u>Sulphur</u> isotope and trace metal co
r X-ray fluorescence	1	<u>trace</u> element analysis of some sta
es. The state of art	2	<u>trace</u> element analysis of geologic
Sulphur isotope and	3	<u>trace</u> metal composition of stratif
mples. Comparison of	1	<u>two</u> background correction procedur
ction procedures for	1	<u>X-ray</u> fluorescence trace element a

Figure 4.2 KWIC index of titles from Fig. 4.1.

Products of Mechanized Retrieval 71

Term	#	Context
ANALYSIS	1	fluorescence trace element analysis of some
ANALYSIS	2	of art trace element analysis of geological
ART	2	The state of art trace element analysis of
BACKGROUND	1	Comparison of two background correction pro
CANADIAN	3	an ore guide in the Canadian Shield. Sulph
COMPARISON	1	Comparison of two background correction pro
COMPOSITION	3	trace metal composition of stratiform sulph
CORRECTION	1	two background correction procedures for X-
DERIVED	2	geological samples as derived from results
ELEMENT	1	fluorescence trace element analysis of some
ELEMENT	2	state of the art trace element analysis of
FLUORESCENCE	1	procedures for X-ray fluorescence trace ele
GEOLOGICAL	2	element analysis of geological samples as d
GUIDE	3	sulphides as an ore guide in the Canadian S
ISOTOPE	3	Shield. Sulphur isotope and trace metal com
METAL	3	isotope and trace metal composition of strat
ORE	3	sulphides as an ore guide in the Canadian Sh
PROCEDURES	1	correction procedures for X-ray fluorescence
RESULTS	2	as derived from results on standard rock sam
ROCK	2	results on standard rock samples. The state
SAMPLES	1	of some standard samples. Comparison of two
SAMPLES	2	on standard rock samples. The state of art
SHIELD	3	in the Canadian Shield. Sulphur isotope an
STANDARD	1	analysis of some standard samples. Comparis
STANDARD	2	from results on standard rock samples. The
STATE	2	rock samples. The state of art trace elemen
STRATIFORM	3	metal composition of stratiform sulphides a
SULPHIDES	3	of stratiform sulphides as an ore guide in
SULPHUR	3	Canadian Shield. Sulphur isotope and trace
TRACE	1	X-ray fluorescence trace element analysis o
TRACE	2	The state of art trace element analysis of
TRACE	3	Sulphur isotope and trace metal composition
TWO	1	Comparison of two background correction pro
X-RAY	1	procedures for X-ray fluorescence trace ele

Figure 4.3   KWOC index of titles from Fig. 4.1.

BEDROCK ANALYSIS	3
CANADIAN SHIELD	3
COPPER ORES	3
EXPLORATION FOR METALS	3
GEOCHEMICAL STANDARDS	1,2
GEOCHEMICAL TECHNIQUES	1,2
GEOMATHEMATICS	1,0
ISOTOPE GEOCHEMISTRY	3
LABORATORY METHODS	1,2
STRATIFORM DEPOSITS	3
ZINC ORES	3

Figure 4.4   Descriptor index to documents listed in Fig. 4.1.

ORE ANALYSIS	1,2,3
TRACE ELEMENTS	1,2,3
X-RAY FLUORESCENCE	1

Figure 4.5   Subject index to documents listed in Fig. 4.1.

Bibliographies

With the correct search instructions, the computer printout can be a bibliography on a given subject, as described in the section Printouts, Tapes above. The years covered by such a bibliography can be set as wished. Bibliographies can also be produced at regular time intervals—e.g., monthly—on subjects of general interest [2], or they may be single-copy, custom-tailored bibliographies for an individual user.

Data Tables

Numerical data can be garnered from certain files such as PROMT [3] and, by using an available program, produced in the form of tables (Fig. 4.6) or even graphs.

Citation Indexes

The Institute of Scientific Information can produce from its SCISEARCH and SOCSEARCH tapes a list of papers in which certain references are cited [4]. This method of linking papers which have cited references in common, developed by Garfield [5], is a most useful method of finding documents on the same scientific topic. Or, in reverse, if a search has been performed on a given subject, the references cited by all the identified papers can be listed to extend the list of references on the subject. Figure 4.7 shows a typical full record from SCISEARCH. The record shown in Fig. 4.7 could have been one of a list of records resulting from a request for all documents citing "Wechsler, D (Messung Intelligence, 1964)." Alternatively, it might have been from a subject search based on the term HAMBURG-WECHSLER-INTELLIGENCE-TEST. A complete bibliography could have been prepared listing the documents found as well as the references cited.

Document Retrieval

Some systems are set up to supply the identified document itself, for example a newspaper article from the New York Times file. The document is usually stored on microfiche. The microfiche may be called up and the image read by cathode ray tube online, or prints may be made and delivered to the user as the product of the search.

INTRODUCTORY SAMPLE

/FREQ(A)

/YRS1 = INTERVAL(1960 to 1977,1980,1985,1990)

/GNP = GETQC(GNP)

/CARS = GETQC(3712S)

/SALES = ENTER(12376,11396,14640,16495,16997,20734,20209,&

/20026,22755,24295,18752,28264,30435,35550,31550,35725)

/TABULATE(YEARS,GNP,CARS,SALES)

YEARS	GNP	CARS	SALES
1960	505.98	6675	12376
1961	523.29	5543	11396
1962	563.82	6933	14640
1963	594.74	7638	16495
1964	635.74	7752	16997
1965	688.11	9305	20734
1966	753.00	8598	20209
1967	796.31	7437	20026
1968	868.47	8822	22755
1969	935.54	8224	24295
1970	982.42	6547	18752
1971	1063.4	8585	28264
1972	1171.1	8824	30435
1973	1306.3	9658	35550
1974	1406.9	7331	31550
1975	1498.8	6713	35725
1976	1685	8300	0
1977	1875	9200	0
1980	2338	10800	0
1985	3275	11500	0
1990	4535	12400	0

/SALESPRO = FORECAST(SALES,GNP,CARS,YEARS: 1976,1977,1980,1985, &

/1990: 1960 to 1975)

R-SQUARED = .98279

Figure 4.6 From "Computational Systems Commands" from Predicasts. (Reproduced with permission from Predicasts, Inc.)

615774   ARTICLE   OATS   ORDER #: BJ618   7 REFS
DIAGNOSTIC SIGNIFICANCE OF SCORES IN MENTAL DEGENERATION IN
HAMBURG-WECHSLER-INTELLIGENCE-TEST   (GE)
   HUNJER J, KLEIM J: NERVENARTZ, V47, N3, P198-200, 1976
   UNIV HAMBURG, NEUROL KLIN, MARTINI STR 52D-2000 HAMBURG//FED REP GER

   ANDERSON AL   (J CLIN PSYCHOLOG, V6, P191, 1950)
   BAXA W   (WIEN Z NERVENHEILK, V30, P119, 1972)
   DAHL G   (PSYCHOL FORSCHUNG, V28, P476, 1965)
   HENNING W   (25 K DTSCH GES PSYCH, 1967)
   KINZEL W   (SCHWEIZ Z PSYCHOL, V33, P115, 1974)
   MAYER K   (DTSCH Z NERVENHEILK, V196, P331, 1969)
   WECHSLER D   (MESSUNG INTELLIGENCE, 1964)

Figure 4.7 Complete record from SCISEARCH, produced by the Institute of Scientific Information. (Reproduced with permission.)

BIBLIOGRAPHIES

The Bibliographic Citation

A bibliography consists of a listing of papers, monographs, books, and reviews relating to a particular subject. The subject area may be broad or narrow. Each citation should identify completely the author and source, so that the original document can be easily found. Figure 4.8 shows several accepted methods of listing a citation. Factors which influence the usefulness of a bibliography are its size, the number of journals and publications examined, the time span, the closeness of fit to the subject, and the harmony with the purpose of the bibliography.

Size of the Bibliography

The size of a bibliography is a function of the breadth of the subject, that is, the amount that has been published on the subject. A complete bibliography on the subject "electron microscopy," a broad subject which includes the technology of electron microscopes as well as their use in many scientific fields, would be huge. The bibliography would cover, for example, what has been done in medicine, mineralogy, and many other fields, and would be hundreds of references long. A bibliography on the subject "metallurgical applications of scanning electron microscopy" would be smaller because the subject has been narrowed by two restrictions, one the field of application (metallurgy) and one the kind of electron microscope (scanning). For the last ten years, there would be perhaps 350 references. The subject "use of scanning electron microscopy to determine size ranges in powdered metals," limited to the last ten years, would produce an even smaller bibliography since it is restricted not only to a subset of metallurgy—powdered metals—but to a subset of powdered metals—their size is the only quality of interest. A good yield would be 35 references.

A number limit can be placed on a bibliography. Many information retrieval centers limit their output, for instance to an arbitrary limit of 100 references. The logical, and cost-effective, way to perform such a limitation is to edit backwards from the current date until 100 references have been identified. For the general subject "electron microscopy," such a list, even though it covers only two or three years, would be adequate because each of the 100 documents would probably cite papers previously published. For a bibliography of a usable size precise definition of the interest when presenting a subject for mechanical searching is necessary. For broad subjects, size limits may be set.

The Time Span

The time span covered by the search will naturally make a difference in the number of documents identified. For most searches, the user would like

Bibliographies

1. Shumaker, C. B.; Fulrath, R. M. Initial Stages of Sintering of Cu and Ni. Material Science Research, Vol. 6, Sintering and Related Phenomena, pp. 191-199 Plenum Press 1973.

2. C. B. Shumaker and R. M. Fulrath, Initial Stages of Sintering of Cu and Ni. Material Science Research; Vol. 6, Sintering and Related Phenomena, Plenum Press 1973 pp. 191-199.

3. Initial Stages of Sintering of Cu and Ni. Shumaker, C. B. and Fulrath, R. M. Material Science Research Vol. 6, Sintering and Related Phenomena, Plenum Press. 1973 pp 191-199.

4. Plenum Press, 1973. Shumaker, C. B. and Fulrath, R. M. INITIAL STAGES OF SINTERING OF CU AND NI. pp. 191-199 of Vol. 6, Sintering and Related Phenomena, of Material Science Research.

5. C. B. Shumaker and R. M. Fulrath
    INITIAL STAGES OF SINTERING OF CU AND NI.
        Material Science Research Vol. 6, Sintering and Related Phenomena, Plenum Press. 1973 pp 191-199

6. C. B. Shumaker and R. M. Fulrath
    INITIAL STAGES OF SINTERING OF CU AND NI.
    Material Science Research. Vol. 6 Sintering and Related Phenomena
    Plenum Press 1973 pp. 191-199

7. Shumaker, C. B., Fulrath, R. M. Material Science Research, Vol. 6, pp 191-199 Plenum Press 1973

Figure 4.8 Acceptable bibliographic citations.

to have references up to the date he receives the bibliography. Manual efforts can be made to approach this goal as closely as possible. Some files will have more recent publications than others; the minimum time lag between publication of a reference and its appearance on the file is roughly 3 months. Strong efforts are made to have the published paper accessioned by the secondary journal or tape a maximum of 6 months after publication. Occasionally, the time lag may be as much as 1 or 2 years.

For most technical and scientific subjects there will be a peak year of publication, because of the changing currents of interest in the flow of scientific knowledge. Original scientific studies, such as those about recombinant genes, will spawn many papers. Government regulations may trigger the publication of technical solutions to problems such as pollution control. A usable search from the user's point of view should include the peak publication years. Figure 4.9 diagrams different ways in which the number of publications may vary with time.

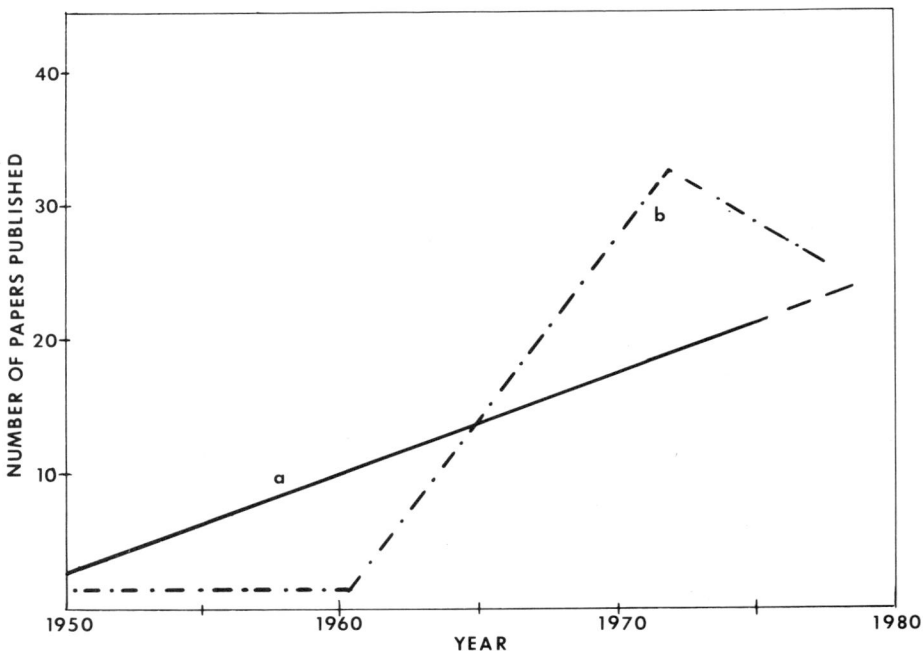

Figure 4.9 Variations in the number of articles published on a given subject as a function of the year of publication. Line a represents a subject of continuing interest, showing the effect of "publish or perish" stimulation. Line b represents a subject such as prostaglandins in which a sudden surge of interest occurs.

Bibliographies 77

At the present time, technical and scientific literature much older than 10 to 12 years is not available on tape. If the information scientist plans to read relevant documents and prepare a report, such as a state-of-the-art report, it may be enough to search 2 to 5 years mechanically, and to rely on cited references from important documents to extend the bibliography. The peak publication years should not be omitted from the mechanical search. As has been said before, a bibliography which is too large to handle in the time available to the user is practically worthless.

Closeness of Fit

The closeness of the fit of the bibliography to the subject of interest is important. Even when the search is as effective as is possible by mechanical means, the printout should be edited. If the printout consists of bibliographic citations only, with no abstracts or notation of contents, it is of course usually impossible to tell which documents are useful. Nevertheless, there will always be false drops which should be edited out. For instance, if a search is about navigational bearings, false drops may occur on the subject of fruit-bearing trees or roller bearings. Besides false drops, other bases can be used for editing, for example language, although the removal of documents in certain languages is unusual when good translations and translating services are available. Most users choose to be aware of information in languages which they cannot read. Another important editing basis, as discussed in Chap. 3, is a third subject modifier applied by manual editing to the results of a two-way subject search.

One page from a three-page computer printout resulting from a mechanized search of the narrow subject "use of scanning electron microscopy to determine size ranges in metal powders" is shown in Fig. 4.10. The printout could have been printed-out in different sequences as discussed above, perhaps the most useful being in reverse order by date of publication. The printout shown in Fig. 4.10 is from a program that prints out the most recent file additions first, resulting in a roughly reverse chronological order.

The Boolean strategy which was used to produce the printout in Fig. 4.10 was

(SCANNING ELECTRON + ELECTRON PROBE ANALYSIS) * (METAL POWDERS + PARTICLE SIZE + POWDER COMPACTS + POWDER METALLURGY + PARTICLE SIZE DISTRIBUTION + POWDER TECHNOLOGY)

Figure 4.11 shows the bibliography as edited by the information scientist who phrased the inquiry in collaboration with the client. The client has requested that the results be limited to metallic powders, so A 34845 is eliminated. The two-way strategy would certainly produce hits about non-metallic powders. The information scientist is also aware that the English

A14612 APPLICATION OF THE SCANNING ELECTRON MICROSCOPE IN THE EXAMINATION OF POWDERS.

I.L. ROIKH, N.A. LITOVCHENKO, S.G. BELITSKAYA, L.G. EGOROVA AND A.S. SAKHIEV

SOV. POWDER METALL. MET. CERAM., OCT. 1972, 11, (10), 777-780.

MET POWDRS   METALLOGRAPHY   PARTICLE SIZE
SCANNING ELECTRON

A18888 INITIAL STAGES OF SINTERING OF CU AND NI.

C.B. SHUMAKER AND R.M. FULRATH

MATERIAL SCIENCE RESEARCH. VOL. 6. SINTERING AND RELATED PHENOMENA, PLENUM PRESS 1973, 191-199

COPPER   HOT STAGE MICROS   METALLOGRAPHY
NICKEL   POWDER COMPACTS   SCANNING ELEC
SINTERING

A24611 DIRECT OBSERVATION OF OPEN POROSITY NETWORKS.

R.M. STRAUSS

METALLOGRAPHY, OCT. 1972, 5, (5), 457-458

AUSTENITIC STAINLE   METALLOGRAPHY   POROSITY
POWDER METALLURGY   SCANNING ELECTR   SPECIMEN PREP

A25702 USE OF THE SCANNING ELECTRON MICROSCOPE FOR STUDYING POWDERS.

I.L. ROIKH, N.A. LITOVCHENKO, S.G. BELITSKAYA, L.G. EGOROVA AND A.S. SAKHNEV

POROSHKOVAYA MET., OCT. 1972, (10), 6-10 (RUSSIAN)

METAL POWDERS   METALLOGRAPHY   PARTICLE SIZE
SCANNING ELECTRON

A34845 SEM STUDY OF METALLOGRAPHIC POLISHING ALUMINAS.

T.G. GREGORY, AND D.R. SCHUYLER

METALLOGRAPHY   APR. 1972   5, --2--, 195-199

ALUMINUM OXIDE   PARTICLE SIZE   PARTICLE SIZE DIST
POLISHING/METALLO   SCANNING ELECTRON

Figure 4.10 Computer printout for "use of scanning electron microscopy to determine size ranges in metal powders."

"Use of Scanning Electron Microscopy
to Determine Size Ranges in Metal Powders"

A18888   INITIAL STAGES OF SINTERING OF CU AND NI.

C. B. Shumaker and R. M. Fulrath.

Material Science Research. Vol. 6 Sintering and Related Phenomena, Plenum Press 1973 pp. 191-199.

A14612   APPLICATION OF THE SCANNING ELECTRON MICROSCOPE IN THE EXAMINATION OF POWDERS.

I. L. Roikh, N. A. Litovchenko, S. G. Belitskaya, L. G. Egorova and A. S. Sakhiev.

Sov. Powder Metall. Met. Ceram., Oct. 1972, 11, (10) pp. 777-780.

A24611   DIRECT OBSERVATION OF OPEN POROSITY NETWORKS.

R. M. Strauss

Metallography, Oct. 1972, 5, (5), pp. 462-465.

Figure 4.11   Bibliography edited from computer printout [see (Fig. 4.10)].

translation version (A 14612) of the Russian article (A 25702) is sufficient reference for the client. When a mechanized search has resulted in a printout consisting of bibliographic citations (title, authors, source, keywords) as shown in Fig. 4.10, the best output that can be forwarded to the client, if it is not considered necessary to examine the original documents, is the edited bibliography shown in Fig. 4.11.

Purpose of the Bibliography

The purpose of the bibliography will have an important bearing on the editing process. If the purpose of the bibliography is to present as complete a listing as possible of all that has been published on a subject, then editing should not remove anything that *may* be relevant. If the bibliography is intended to list recent publications on the subject of interest so that the user can bring himself up to date, older publications can be edited out, as can publications in hard-to-get or obscure journals. Review and book entries should be retained.

BIBLIOGRAPHIES WITH ABSTRACTS

Some mechanical files carry abstracts of the documents, and where these are available they may be printed out. If abstracts are not on the tape they may appear in the matching hard-copy abstract journal, if one exists. Usually the original document will include an abstract by the author. If the publication is not a professional journal, however, there may be no abstract. If there is none, the information scientist may be asked to provide one for his client. Instructions for writing abstracts are given in [6] and [7]. While expertise in the subject is useful in the preparation of an abstract, a reasonably good abstract can often be prepared from the original document by using first and last sentences from paragraphs and some intelligent commonsense. If the original document cannot be understood by the abstractor, he should not attempt to abstract. When an abstract is prepared from a document, care should be exercised not to rearrange or substitute for the original author's words. The goal should be a shortened resumé of the article as written. Clarification may be needed, but should be attempted only when it is obviously essential and when it is within the abstractor's capabilities.

If the abstracts are given with the bibliography it is possible to categorize. A portion of such a product is shown in Appendix I (page 84).

ANNOTATED BIBLIOGRAPHIES

Annotated bibliographies are often of use, when the annotations are based on some user-requested orientation. The annotation can be as simple as a note that the work in question is part of a research direction characteristic of a certain group of investigators, or as elaborate as an analysis of the whole background of a problem as revealed by the approaches of a number of authors. Figure 4.12 is an example of a short annotated bibliography.

STRUCTURED REFERENCE LISTINGS

As mentioned at the beginning of this chapter, the computer can be programmed to sequence the items in the printout in various ways. For example, the documents can be listed by date of publication, the most recent first. By the use of index term combinations they can be listed in groups from the most relevant to the least relevant. As so programmed, the

Structured Reference Listings

---

14. Wegner, Peter, Editor, INTRODUCTION TO SYSTEM PROGRAMMING. Academic Press, New York, 1964. 316 pp

15. International Computation Center, Rome, SYMBOLIC LANGUAGES IN DATA PROCESSING. Gordon and Breach, New York, 1962. 849 pp

   These two volumes are collections of articles on programming systems. Over 90% of them deal with procedure oriented language and their translators-compilers.

16. Halstead, Maurice H., MACHINE-INDEPENDENT COMPUTER PROGRAMS. Spartan Books, Washington D.C., 1962 267 pp.

   This volume discusses the construction of a specific compiler for a specific language, NELIAC, which is a version of ALGOL. Since many of the principles set forth here are general in nature and clearly presented, this is a valuable book for anyone who finds it necessary to write a compiler.

Figure 4.12 Annotated bibliography. Ivan Flores, COMPUTER SOFTWARE, © 1965, p. 474. Reprinted by permission of Prentice-Hall, Inc.

printout will be "raw" computer output, but nevertheless a good starting point for an edited structured bibliography.

An example of a structured bibliography is the "Project Profile" prepared by The Knowledge Availability Systems Center at the University of Pittsburgh. After reading titles and (where available) abstracts, the information scientist writes a résumé of the search results, including an in-depth discussion of the original query and an explanation of the reasons for the categorization of the results. Sometimes the information scientist will find it necessary to read one or two of the original documents, or to supplement the mechanical search by a manual search in the library, but usually neither is done since such activities would double or triple the time spent on the profile.

A new approach to the structured bibliography, called a Biblio-Profile, has recently been reported by Lois F. Lunin [8] from the Information Center for Hearing, Speech and Disorders of Human Communication of the Johns

Hopkins Medical Institutions. The Biblio-Profile presents a short background resumé on the subject followed by a comprehensive bibliography. The background discussions are solicited from experts by the information center. The center provides a search to the expert, and itself prepares the Biblio-Profile bibliography from the search.

DIGESTS AND REVIEWS

Digests and reviews will give the user a much better base from which to judge the usefulness of the referenced documents than will a bibliography. Digests and reviews do more than summarize the contents of documents. A digest may be a critical analysis of the contents of one or more documents, and a review may be a critical analysis of all the recent documents considered to be of value on the subject of the review. Digests and reviews should be prepared by individuals with at least a good background in the subject considered. If the individual has much knowledge in the particular field being reviewed, so much the better, as little or no background study will be necessary to get the correct perspective. The best advice to the writer of a review or digest is to stick to the facts as presented and not to "fake" or to make assumptions. Appendix II (page 88) is an example of a digest of one article.

REPORTS

The results of a literature survey, and the analysis of these results, are often included within another publication such as a proposal or a technical report of a research project. Quite frequently, however, the results of the literature survey will stand alone as a state-of-the-art report. Such a report is usually written by an acknowledged expert in the field. A group of guidelines useful for writing such a report are as follows:

1. Explain the purpose of the literature search.
2. From the purpose, make clear the search plan and the plan for presentation of the results.
3. Give a list of _useful_ references. There is no need to give all the references, since it is the reporter's duty to screen them for the user.

Much has been written to help the writer of technical reports. A few references are given in [9-16].

Appendix III (page 89) is an example of a report on a literature survey, selected because it is short enough to be included here. Most reports of literature surveys are on broader subjects and are therefore considerably longer.

SPECIAL FILES

Machine Readable Results

An individual or a company may request that the results of a literature search be machine-readable—i.e., on magnetic tape or on punched cards. For example, a chemical firm may request monthly updates on a number of queries. If the results of the searches are machine-readable, printouts can be circulated monthly as received to the chemists in the firm who originated the queries. The machine-readable results can then be merged into the company's reference files. The machine-readable results must be compatible with the client company's computer system and must be designed so that they can be printed out from the client's computer in the pattern desired. For example, if the client wants to print out results with the year of publication of the document always appearing at a given place on the printout, then the year of publication must appear on the tape as a separate record—that is, not as an inseparable member of a larger record incorporating the volume, the month, and the page.

Results in Microform

Results may also be provided to the client company as microform, either of abstracts or of full documents. If the microform is aperture cards or microfiche it may be edge-notched for filing and searching. Film, usually 35 mm, may be stored in cartridges. The cartridges will be labeled and the film itself marked or coded so that the needed information may be found quickly by using a reading machine such as the Recordak. Reference [17] will give further information about handling microforms.

Management Information Files

While this book has been limited to the retrieval of documents about science and technology, some mention should be made of the use of management information files. The primary purpose of such files is to present data, for the most part numerical, in such a way as to give the manager a lucid, to-the-point grasp of the facts of interest. Such a system will produce reports, tabular or graphical. The design of the data base and the available output forms are quite important. References [18] and [19] give an introduction to the subject of designing data bases to give graphical or tabular output. Since science and technology must have reliable data to solve problems, files designed for graphical or tabular presentation of results may come to be the most useful end result of information retrieval.

SUMMARY

The results of a literature search, whether mechanized or manual, appear first as a list of bibliographic citations. Such a list may be presented as the final result of the search, or it may be supplemented by abstracts or notes. It may also be presented arranged by subject, alphabetically by author, or chronologically.

The size of the bibliography, and—a related quantity—the time span covered, should be controlled. Good journal and publication coverage should be insured by careful selection of the files to be searched. The raw computer output should be edited to assure closeness of fit to the subject and to the purpose of the bibliography.

Literature search results may also be presented as digests of document contents and as reviews of the subject as ascertained from examination of the referenced documents. Literature search results may also be given to the client as special tapes, files of microforms, or data on the form of special mechanized files programmed to produce tables or graphs in answer to queries.

APPENDIX I Example of a Categorized Bibliography*

Technology of Solar Energy Collectors

FEASIBILITY DEMONSTRATION OF A SOLAR POWERED TURBO-COMPRESSOR AIR CONDITIONING AND HEATING SYSTEM.

United Aircraft Research Labs., East Hartford, Conn.
*National Science Foundation, Washington, D.C.
Research Applied to National Needs. (357-370)

Quarterly progress rept. no. 1, 15 Jun-15 Sep 74
AUTHOR: Biancardi, F. R.
C4234G2   FLD: 10B, 97C   USGRDR7507
15 Sep 74   48p
RET NO: UARL-N951923-1
CONTRACT: NSF-C903
MONITOR: NSF/RA/N-74-105

---

*The references and abstracts contained in this appendix have been reproduced from the government files, National Technical Information Service (NTIS), and National Aeronautics and Space Administration (NASA).

Appendix I 85

ABSTRACT: This report describes work performed to demonstrate the feasibility of operating a Rankine cycle turbocompressor air conditioning and heating system at temperature levels consistent with present-day flat-plate solar collectors. The specific objectives of the program are (1) to demonstrate, through the testing of an existing turbocompressor system modified for the application, that such a system can be operated easily, efficiently, and safely at temperature levels achievable with present-day collectors and (2) to demonstrate through sufficient analyses and testing that future commercial versions of such a system have the potential for low-cost fabrication and efficient operation required for commercial application of the system. Primary emphasis was placed on defining the operating conditions of components and selecting the working fluid for the demonstration turbocompressor system. Emphasis was also placed on the disassembly and check of the existing turbocompressor components, and the modification or procurement of new components required for the laboratory demonstrator.

GUIDE FOR CALCULATING COLLECTION EFFICIENCY FOR THE SHALLOW SOLAR POND (APPLICABLE FOR ANY HORIZONTAL FLAT PLATE SOLAR COLLECTOR).

W. C. Dickinson and R. D. Neifert.

California Univ. Livermore. Lawrence Livermore Lab.
1 feb. 1974   44 p.   refs. (Contract W-7405-eng-48)
(UCID-16446)   Avail. NTIS   HG $4.25

The Collection efficiency of a solar collector system was calculated by a method of Hottel and Whillier and Liu and Jordan. The method calculated the hourly rate of energy collection and the long term on monthly average collection efficiency based upon monthly average daily solar insolation data and daytime temperatures obtained from Weather Bureau data. The method provides the most realistic values of collection efficiency that can be obtained for a given collector system in a given location. Not only is the monthly variation taken into account but also the statistical effect of bad weather. A computer program was written to calculate average hourly values of collected heat and average daily values of collection efficiency.

Materials Used for Solar Collectors

PLEXIGLAS DR THERMAL STABILITY TEST.

Alan P. Saunders

National Center for Energy Management and Power,
Philadelphia, Pa. *National Science Foundation,
Washington, D. C. Research Applied to National Needs.
*Towne School of Civil and Mechanical Engineering,
Philadelphia, Pa. Technical rept. 14 Aug. 72   7p
Rept. No.: NSF/RANN/SR/GI27976/TR/72/4

Plexiglas DR (a Rohm and Haas extrudable methyl methacrylate) used as the inner sheet in a non-operating double-pane solar collector exposed to summer solar radiation suffers major distortions. This material is not suitable for use in this environment unless the collectors are shielded from the sun during collector shutdown.

CONSERVATION AND BETTER UTILIZATION OF ELECTRIC POWER BY MEANS OF THERMAL ENERGY STORAGE AND SOLAR HEATING. PHASE IV.

Hsuan Yeh

Progress rept. National Center for Energy Management and Power, Philadelphia, Pa. *National Science Foundation, Washington, D. C. Research Applied to National Needs. 30 Jun 73 19p
Rept. No. NSF/RANN/SE/GI27976/PR/73/2

A brief review of work on off-peak air conditioning, materials for thermal energy storage, and solar collectors is presented.

Residential Solar Collectors

THE DEVELOPMENT OF A SOLAR POWERED RESIDENTIAL HEATING AND COOLING SYSTEM. FINAL REPORT.

Mark J. O'Neill, Paul O. McCormick, and William R. Kruse

Lockheed Missiles and Space C. Huntsville Ala.
Research and Engineering Center   1974   95p. refs.
NASA-CR-120400

A solar energy collector design is disclosed that would be efficient for both energy transfer and fluid flow, based upon extensive parametric analyses. Thermal design requirements are generated for the energy storage systems which utilize sensible heat storage in water. Properly sized system components (including the collector and storage) and a practical efficient total system configuration are determined by means of computer simulation of system performance.

Appendix I

THE DEVELOPMENT OF A SOLAR-POWERED RESIDENTIAL HEATING AND COOLING SYSTEM.

no author

National Aeronautics and Space Administration,
Marshall Space Flight Center, Huntsville, Ala.
NASA-TM-X-70089

Efforts to demonstrate the engineering feasibility of utilizing solar power for residential heating and cooling are described. These efforts were concentrated on the analysis, design, and test of a full-scale demonstration system which is currently under construction at the National Aeronautics and Space Administration Marshall Space Flight Center, Huntsville, Alabama. The basic solar heating and cooling system under development utilizes a flat plate solar energy collector, a large water tank for thermal energy storage, heat exchangers for space heating and water heating, and an absorption cycle air conditioner for space cooling.

Reviews

SOLAR HEATING AND AIR CONDITIONING (A BIBLIOGRAPHY WITH ABSTRACTS)

Audrey S. Hundemann

Rept. for 1964-Dec. 74. Supercedes COM-74-11103
C4232A3 National Technical Information Service, Springfield, Va.

Presented are 71 abstracts pertaining to solar heating and cooling of buildings. Abstracts cover reports dealing primarily with technical feasibility. Included are a few abstracts of reports on solar energy as a national energy resource; solar energy research program alternatives; and economic, social, environmental, and institutional factors affecting the feasibility of using solar energy for heating and cooling buildings.

USE OF SOLAR ENERGY IN BUILDINGS IN NEW YORK STATE.

Clyde G. Oakley

New York State Assembly Scientific Staff, Albany
*National Science Foundation, Washington, D. C.
Office of Intergovernmental Science and Research

Utilization* Syracuse Univ., N.Y. Dept. of Electrical
and Computer Engineering. Final rept. Oct. 73-Apr. 74.
Rept. No. SS-405   Grant NSF-ISR72-05606-A02

A brief History of solar energy use is given and potential advantages and disadvantages of using solar energy are examined. Report presents an overview of solar devices and discusses two common types of solar cells and other parts of a solar electrical system. The impact of increased use of solar heating and cooling and factors that have discouraged use of solar energy are discussed along with possible actions the New York State Legislature could take concerning solar energy.

APPENDIX II   Example of a Digest*

Electroplating Titanium

Titanium alloys can be plated by wet blasting, plating electroless nickel, heat bonding and electroplating.

Titanium and its alloys require metallic coatings to eliminate galling and seizing, improve electrical conductivity or solderability, and provide corrosion and oxidation resistance. To produce such coating, electroless nickel is used as an intermediate base. It can be bonded by heat treatment and electroplated with adherent layers of gold and other metals.

Etching in hot concentrated solutions of hydrochloric acid, recommended before electroless nickel plating, is satisfactory for unalloyed titanium, but unsatisfactory for B120VCA because of the large quantity of hydrogen which the alloy absorbs.

However, wet blasting (with 1000 mesh glass beads or 1250 mesh silica) before plating with electroless nickel develops a usable surface. Subsequently, the titanium is activated in an acid solution containing nickel chloride. To bond the nickel, the plated titanium is heated at 750-1000°F in argon.

An acid or alkaline solution containing nickel sulfate or nickel chloride and sodium hypophosphite can be used for plating electroless nickel. In either case, the reduction of nickel ions must be initiated by making the titanium a cathode. This is done by momentarily coupling it with a very active metal, such as aluminum, or by impressing direct current upon it. A nickel thickness of 0.02 mil is regarded as minimum and a range of 0.1 to 0.3 mil is recommended.

---

* Reproduced from Metal Progress, July 1964, pp. 167-168.

Appendix III

After the nickel plate is bonded, the surface is scrubbed with pumice. Gold is plated in a solution of potassium cyanide and gold cyanide or potassium cyanide and citric acid. The hydrogen content of titanium alloy specimens electroplated in this manner was 69 ppm; this is considerably less than the 350 ppm level which causes embrittlement. The resulting plate adheres to the nickel substrate and the B120VCA alloy satisfactorily.

Digested by William H. Safranek from William B. Harding. "Electroplating on Titanium and Titanium Alloys," Plating 1963, 131-135.

APPENDIX III Example of Report of Literature Review*

Cu-Se Copper-Selenium

Reference [1] indicates that at elevated temperatures Cu_2Se exists over the range 33.3-35.6 a/o Se, the structure being FCC, CaF_2 type. The Se-rich limit is set by [2] at 35 a/o Se. At the Se-rich end of this miscibility zone, i.e., between 35 and 35.6 a/o Se, the FCC structure is retained to room temperature, according to [1]. However, at the Cu-rich end a number of low-temperature inversions can be encountered, depending on the heating and cooling history. According to [3], no less than seven different crystal structures can be identified. These are either BCC or tetragonal types with different lattice parameters. Obviously, most of these are metastable. The truly stable low-temperature structure probably cannot be established at this point. [4] give the melting point of Cu_2Se as 1148 ± 5°C from differential thermal-analysis data.

Although Cu_2Se could be distinguished in phase mixtures with Cu_2Se and CuSe, [1] were unable to synthesize a single-phase structure. The compound $CuSe_2$ is reported by [1], but its structure was not determined. [5], investigating thin films formed by vapor deposition, concluded that CuSe is less stable than $Cu_{2-x}Se$.

1. W. Borchert and I. Patzak, Heidelb. Beitr. Mineral. Petrogr. 4, 1955, 434-442.
2. A. Boettcher, G. Haase, and H. Treupel. Z. Angew. Physik 7, 1955, 478-487.
3. G. Lorenz and C. Wagner. J. Chem. Phys. 26, 1957, 1607-1608.

---

*From Constitution of Binary Alloys, First Supplement. Rodney P. Elliott, Editor. Copyright 1965 by McGraw-Hill Book Company. Used with permission of McGraw-Hill Book Company.

4. D. R. Mason and D. F. O'Kane. International Conference on Semiconductor Physics, Prague, 1960. Academic Press Inc., New York, 1961, pp. 1026-1031.
5. G. A. Efendiev and M. M. Kazinets. Izv. Akad. Nauk Azerb. SSR, Ser. Fiz.-Mat. Tekhn. Nauk, 1960(5), 91-98.

REFERENCES

1. K. H. Baser, S. M. Cohen, D. L. Dayton, and P. B. Watkins. "Online Indexing Experiment at Chemical Abstracts Service: Algorithmic Generation of Articulated Index Entries from Natural Language Phrases." J. Chem. Inf. Comput. Sci. 18n(1), 1978, 18.
2. Chemical Abstracts Service. CA Selects. Columbus, Ohio.
3. Predicasts, Inc., Cleveland, Ohio.
4. Richard Sweet. "User's Guide to Online Searching of SCISEARCH and and Social SCISEARCH." Lockheed DIALOG Retrieval Service, Palo Alto, Calif.
5. E. Garfield. "Citation Indexes for Science." Science 122(3159), July 15 1955, 108.
6. Chemical Abstracts Service. Directions for Abstractors. Columbus, Ohio, 1975.
7. David R. Krathwohl. How to Prepare a Research Proposal. Syracuse University Bookstore, Syracuse, New York, 1966.
8. Lois F. Lunin. "The Biblio-Profile - A Two-in-One Package of Information: Its Preparation, Production, Marketing, Uses." J. Amer. Soc. Inf. Sci. 27(2), 1976, 113.
9. Theodore A. Sherman and Simon S. Johnson, Modern Technical Writing Prentice-Hall, Englewood Cliffs, New Jersey, 1975.
10. William L. Rivers. Finding Facts. Prentice-Hall, Englewood Cliffs, New Jersey, 1975.
11. M. L. Manheimer. Style Manual: A Guide for the Preparation of Reports and Dissertations. Marcel Dekker, New York, 1973.
12. William Strunk, Jr. and E. B. White. The Elements of Style. MacMillan, New York, 1972.
13. Joseph N. Ulman, Jr. and Jay R. Gould. Technical Reporting. Holt, Rinehart and Winston, 1972.
14. Margaret Norgaard. A Technical Writer's Handbook. Harper and Brothers, New York, 1959.
15. Kenneth Albert Kobe. Chemical Engineering Reports: How to Search the Literature and Prepare a Report. Interscience, New York, 1957, 35-116.
16. H. J. Tichy. "Engineers Can Write Better." Chem. Eng. Progr. 50, February, April, July, 1954, 104, 206, 365.

References

17. Margaret C. Kolb. "Document Storage and Handling in Information Systems." In Technical Information Center Administration (Arthur W. Elias, Ed.). Spartan Books, Washington, D.C., 1975, 39.
18. Susan Wooldridge. Computer Output Design. Petrocelli/Charter, New York, 1975.
19. James Martin. Principles of Data Base Management. Prentice-Hall, Englewood Cliffs, New Jersey, 1976.

chapter 5
Judging the Results of Mechanized Retrieval

INTRODUCTION

Results of mechanized retrieval may be presented in many ways, as discussed in Chap. 4. The raw computer output may appear in different forms, depending upon what is stored in the computer, what is requested by the search program, and what options are available in the print program. The raw computer output must be examined to judge whether the search has achieved its goal. Attempts have been made to develop algorithms to judge effectiveness. Cost is always a consideration which limits the search, and the effects of this limitation must be considered. If cost considerations render a search ineffective, there is no point in doing the search, and another way of obtaining useful results must be found. User reactions to search results must always be considered, and search procedures modified to make the user happy, if possible.

HOW DO YOU KNOW THE SEARCH WAS EFFECTIVE?

Studies of search effectiveness as first attempted at Western Reserve University defined six measurement factors [1]. These factors were

1. The resolution factor

    $$\frac{\text{Number of retrieved documents}}{\text{Number of documents in system}}$$

2. The elimination factor

    $$\frac{\text{Number of unretrieved documents}}{\text{Number of documents in system}}$$

3. The pertinence factor

    $$\frac{\text{Number of relevant documents retrieved}}{\text{Number of retrieved documents}}$$

How Do You Know the Search Was Effective? 93

4. The noise factor

$$\frac{\text{Number of nonrelevant documents retrieved}}{\text{Number of retrieved documents}}$$

5. The recall factor

$$\frac{\text{Number of relevant documents retrieved}}{\text{Number of relevant documents in system}}$$

6. The omission factor

$$\frac{\text{Number of relevant documents not retrieved}}{\text{Number of relevant documents in system}}$$

Of these only factor 3, now called "precision," and factor 5, the "recall" factor, are studied today.

Recall

In an information search of collections of published literature, the searcher may be looking for every document in the collection that relates to the subject of interest. Sometimes, however, the searcher would like only two or three comprehensive and reliable sources of information about the subject. Sometimes, too, the searcher is pretty sure there is nothing in the collection, or nothing published, about the subject, and wants his belief confirmed. Usually, however, a literature search is instigated to find what has appeared in print about the subject of interest.

A literature searcher then wishes to identify all the documents in the collection which are relevant to the subject of the search. A measure of the search effectiveness, viewed from the simplest point of view, is the ratio of the number of relevant documents retrieved to the total number of relevant documents in the collection. This ratio is called the recall.

$$\text{Recall} = \frac{\text{Number relevant documents retrieved}}{\text{Number relevant documents in the file}}$$

Obviously, unless the file has been artificially prepared as a test file for the purpose of studying the value of different searching techniques, the recall is impossible to measure. If the relevant documents in the file are already known, a search would be unnecessary. Attempts have been made to measure the recall in order to study the effectiveness of search procedures [2,3] but there is no good way to use the recall as a measure of effectiveness.

In practical searching, a recall of less than 1 (where 1 represents complete recall) may become apparent upon the discovery that an item known to be in the file has not been retrieved. When such a discovery is made by a requester and brought to the attention of the information scientist who carried out the search, it can be the cause of heartbreak and bitterness. But when the retrieval of documents containing thousands of words is totally dependent on 3 to 15 index terms, 3 to 10 title words, and up to 50 words of prose in an abstract, it is not surprising that mechanical searching never results in a recall of 1.

Well, almost never. It is possible to set up a search in such broad terms that there is practically a guarantee of full coverage of a narrow interest. But this search becomes, in reality, a manual search of a mechanically produced subfile of the original file. It does not constitute an actual bona fide mechanical search.

There are, of course, requests for information to which the concept of recall does not apply. A request for a fact, such as the melting point of a certain alloy, may be answered by the retrieval of one document, no matter how many relevant ones are in the file. The question of quality may become important, however, with such a request. Has the melting point been determined more accurately by another researcher whose paper was not found by the search? For such a search it is necessary to know with what accuracy the requested data should be provided. Will the figure in the CRC Handbook of Chemistry and Physics be sufficient, or does the user want to know what the latest accurate measurement is?

Precision

A more easily measured estimate of the efficiency of the search is the precision [4]. Precision is the ratio of the number of relevant items retrieved to the total number of items retrieved

$$\text{Precision} = \frac{\text{Number of relevant documents retrieved}}{\text{Number of documents retrieved}}$$

To retrieve a thousand items of which only two or three are relevant appears to be inefficient and a waste of time. If very little has been written on a subject, however, it may sometimes be necessary to retrieve a large number of items in order to find the one or two which are pertinent. In other words, when a large number of relevant items are found, it is acceptable for one or two to slip through the net, but if these one or two are the only relevant documents in the file, then their loss is to be deplored. Low precision may be acceptable for a subject of low expectancy. A corollary is that "nothing has been published" must not be reported after a careless, negligent, or incomplete search.

Usually a low precision is undesirable. On the other hand, if the precision is high—that is, if most of the items retrieved are relevant—the searcher has cause to wonder whether he has retrieved all the relevant items in the file.

How Do You Know the Search Was Effective? 95

Theoretically, the most desirable situation is a precision between 0.3 and 0.7. Table 5.1 shows such a situation when the search is well balanced. Table 5.2 shows how such a precision figure can be misleading, with far less of the relevant documents actually retrieved. A search can be unbalanced in its direction, so that while some relevant documents are found many others lie in a direction not approached by the strategy.

Dependent as automated literature searching is upon alphabetical terms for which there are many possible synonyms, and for which precision meanings may be camouflaged by more general descriptions, and upon the presence of terms from different definitive concepts, it is truly an art to achieve a good search.

TABLE 5.1 Postulated Efficient Search of a 500 Document File

	Numbers of documents		
	Relevant	Not relevant	Total
Retrieved	30	20	50
Not retrieved	10	440	450
Total	40	460	500

Precision = 30/50 = 0.60
Recall   = 30/40 = 0.75

TABLE 5.2 Postulated Search Which Failed to Net Most of the Relevant Items

	Numbers of documents		
	Relevant	Not relevant	Total
Retrieved	30	20	50
Not retrieved	70	380	450
Total	100	400	500

Precision = 30/50 = 0.60
Recall   = 30/100 = 0.30

System Capabilities as Functions of Recall and Precision

The efficiency of mechanized retrieval of information can vary greatly from one system to another. The "system" must be thought of as including the searcher and his relative abilities. Table 5.3 represents two searches of a file with 2000 documents altogether, 50 of which are relevant to the search entered. Two different approaches, one yielding 100 documents and one yielding 1000 documents, are imagined. For the 100-document retrieval, assuming that the file contains 50 pertinent documents, the recall would be 30/50 or 0.6 and the precision 30/100 or 0.3. For the 1000-document retrieval, the recall would be 32/50 or 0.64 and the precision 32/1000 or 0.032. While a precision of 0.3 is not optimum, a precision of 0.03 is far too low to indicate an efficient search. It is by means of the precision figure that the efficiency of the search can be judged.

Further indication of the use of precision to judge the validity of the search is shown in Table 5.4. The subject of the investigation in this table may be assumed to be something along the lines of "the attack of a special steel by HCl in a humid atmosphere." It is obvious that such a search is much more difficult than a simple request for information on the subject of the corrosion of steel. In Table 5.4, it is assumed that the file contains 70 pertinent documents and goes back to 1974. Strategy 1 was oriented toward the behavior of the special steel in humid atmospheres, while strategy 2

TABLE 5.3 Two Approaches to a 2000-Document File, One Narrow, One Broad

	Numbers of documents		
	Relevant	Not relevant	Total
Narrow			
Retrieved	30	70	100
Not retrieved	20	1880	1900
Total	50	1950	2000
Precision = 30/100 = 0.30			
Recall = 30/50 = 0.60			
Broad			
Retrieved	32	968	1000
Not retrieved	18	982	1000
Total	50	1950	2000
Precision = 32/1000 = 0.032			
Recall = 32/50 = 0.64			

TABLE 5.4 Effect of Different Strategies on Precision and Recall[a]

Back to the year	Number of documents retrieved	Number of pertinent documents	Precision	Recall	Cost in dollars
Strategy 1 (optimum)					
1977	50	22	0.44	0.31	5
1976	100	40	0.40	0.57	10
1975	150	54	0.36	0.77	15
1974	200	63	0.32	0.90	20
Strategy 2 (too broad)					
1977	100	22	0.22	0.31	10
1976	200	40	0.20	0.57	20
1975	300	54	0.18	0.77	30
1974	400	63	0.16	0.90	40
Strategy 3 (warped)					
1977	50	11	0.22	0.15	5
1976	100	20	0.20	0.29	10
1975	150	27	0.18	0.39	15
1974	200	32	0.16	0.46	20

[a] Costs are based on cost of abstract prints only at 10¢ an abstract. Total number of pertinent documents in the file is 70.

was oriented toward the attack of the special steel by HCl. Strategy 3 is postulated to be similar to strategy 1 but lacks some essential terms in the strategy. The precision figures of strategy 1 seem to indicate a consistency and a precision that is about all that can be hoped for in an ordinary mechanical search. The precision figures for strategy 2 are low as are those for strategy 3. Judging from these figures, if the precisions are low then the strategy is either too broad, is not oriented in the right direction, or the logic relationships are too loose or untrue. Of the suggested strategies, it is probable that strategy 2 is retrieving much information about the attack of the steel by corrosive atmospheres made up of large percentages of HCl, while the information derived from strategy 1 is about the behavior of the steel in humid atmospheres containing HCl. The relative importance of the search concepts should be considered when a search seems unsuccessful, that is, has a low precision.

A situation could exist where the precision is high but the search is incomplete. Such a possibility is demonstrated in Table 5.5. It is postulated that the searched file contains 1000 relevant documents. This is an example

TABLE 5.5 Results of a Tight Strategy

Back to the year	Number of documents retrieved	Number of pertinent documents	Precision	Recall	Cost in dollars
1977	50	40	0.8	0.04	5
1976	100	80	0.8	0.08	10
1975	200	160	0.8	0.16	20
1974	500	400	0.8	0.40	50

of a strategy which is too tight. A broader strategy, while resulting in lower precision, would be more sure of finding all the relevant documents. The results of this broadened strategy might be as shown in Table 5.6. In the far right-hand column of Tables 5.5 and 5.6 is listed the cost of the retrieved search, at a price of 10 cents an abstract with no other costs considered. It is apparent from Table 5.5 that more pertinent abstracts per unit cost can be purchased with the narrower strategy.

A cost approach may deprive the user of much information. Unfortunately, a high precision-low recall yield does not mean that the cream of the file has been skimmed. Arguments for the narrow, precise strategy do not take into account possible lack of precision in the indexing or the titles.

The number of items retrieved, as shown in Tables 5.4, 5.5, and 5.6, may be a function of how far back in time the search extends. Files are usually searched so that the most recent documents are printed first. A request to print fifty documents then results in the most recent fifty in the file. Sometimes publication on a subject peaks at a certain time—more is published on a subject in a certain year—for example, because of the "jump on the bandwagon" effect or because of the occurrence of a natural phenomenon—sunspots, eclipses, etc. Table 5.7 shows the effect of a peak of publication around 1975 on the precision and recall for searches extending back to certain years. While the figures here show a realistic jump in precision for the peak year, such a jump in precision may not occur since it will depend upon how well the subject terms of the strategy fit the subject terms of the documents published in the peak year.

Not only strategy preparation but also indexing has an effect on precision and recall. When the file is indexed by a closed coordinated index (see Chap. 3), recall is good, provided the indexing terms are precise to the subject of interest. If the index terms of such a closed index system are small in number and generic in meaning, the precision may not be high for searches based on less generic concepts. When free-text indexing is available—that is, all meaningful terms in title, abstract, and/or descriptors are available for searching—greater precision for narrow specific subjects can be obtained. If the subject of the search is general, however, it

TABLE 5.6 Results of a Broad Strategy

Back to the year	Number of documents retrieved	Number of pertinent documents	Precision	Recall	Cost in dollars
1977	300	135	0.45	0.135	30
1976	500	225	0.45	0.225	50
1975	1000	450	0.45	0.45	100
1974	2000	900	0.45	0.90	200

TABLE 5.7 Results for a Subject Having a Peak Year of Publication (1975)

Back to the year	Number of documents retrieved	Number of pertinent documents	Precision	Recall[a]	Cost in dollars
1976	50	20	0.40	0.08	5
1974	260	160	0.62	0.64	40
1972	330	180	0.55	0.72	45
1970	400	200	0.50	0.80	50

[a] Based on the whole file back through January, 1970.

is often a benefit to both precision and recall to select, for instance in Engineering Index, the major headings under which the documents would be expected to fall, and to search for documents which should occur under the appropriate headings. This method applies closed indexing to a file which may be searched free-text as well.

In Chemical Abstracts (CA) files, the numbers of the CA sections where relevant documents would be expected to appear can be used as strategy modifiers, or as means of limiting the amount of output. Output can also be limited by specifying authors, years of publication, or language. Since the size of the output affects the usefulness of the search by fixing both the cost of searching and the time necessary to examine the results, it is usually essential to limit it, the most common way being by years covered. Sometimes the user is interested only in results from a certain group of authors. Sometimes papers published in only certain selected journals are acceptable.

With the advent of online capability for searching files, it has become possible to browse. A search can be initiated, and some of the citations, with or without abstracts, examined directly online. Other relevant search words may be suggested, or an interesting publication by a certain author uncovered. It is then possible to set up the search with the addition of the newly identified words, or to request all papers that are written by the interesting author or that cite the interesting paper.

Coverage of journals by files is an extremely important matter. While on the face of it it seems sufficient to search the Metals file for subjects of a metallurgical nature, other much larger files such as Engineering Index, Chemical Abstracts, and INSPEC may cover journals not covered by the Metals file but still containing peripheral publications of considerable importance to investigators of, for instance, the design of rolling mills, the purification of titanium, or the electrical properties of alloys.

With online searches it is possible to be iterative, that is, to search, examine examples of output, refine the strategy, and re-search. Batch processing may be cheaper and less time-consuming for searches with an established good strategy.

Cost Benefits

A great deal of interest has been shown in the cost benefits of mechanical searching as compared to manual searching [5]. Table 5.8 gives actual figures for some searches made of the Lockheed File in the spring of 1978, during peak daylight hours. Three searches are covered. The first involved searches of five different files, the second of three different files, and the third of only one file. For good coverage of subjects it is often expedient for the searcher to investigate more than one file. The optimum number seems to be about three, but depends of course on the subject. For many searches one file is sufficient. Five files for one search is most unusual, and seems unnecessary for a searcher specializing in one subject, as the searcher should be able to select from knowledge of the files the three which would be most significant. It is also possible online to compare the postings of the several files for different term combinations and to select those files which seem to be most promising.

Table 5.9 is derived by averaging the figures from Table 5.8. From this table it is seen that, for this modest sample chosen as representative of the author's experience with subject searching, the average exhaustive online mechanical search lasts 0.35 hours, produces 167 prints, and costs $54.53. To this cost should be added the cost of the searcher's preparation for the search, which may involve trial searches manually in the library, the reading of applicable references, and the construction of the search strategy. Depending on the salary of the professional who does the preparation, this could amount to $10-$15 per hour.

If we add to the average cost of the mechanical search two hours of preparation time at $10 an hour, the total cost to prepare an average printed bibliography with abstracts by automated retrieval is $74.53. At the same

TABLE 5.8 Actual Figures from Searches of Lockheed Online System

	Estimated total cost, dollars	Search hours	Cost of file, dollars	Cost of tymnet, dollars	Number of prints	Cost of prints, dollars
Search 1						
File 1	19.82	0.223	10.04	1.78	50	8.00
File 2	4.86	0.020	1.30	0.16	34	3.40
File 3	10.57	0.067	6.03	0.54	20	4.00
File 4	43.29	0.056	5.04	0.45	189	37.80
File 5	19.71	0.133	8.65	1.06	100	10.00
Total	98.25	0.499	31.06	3.99	393	63.20
Average	19.65	0.0998	6.212	0.798	78.6	12.64
Search 2						
File 1	1.87	0.016	1.04	0.13	7	0.70
File 2	7.02	0.097	5.34	0.78	9	0.90
File 3	16.98	0.161	14.48	1.29	6	1.20
Total	25.87	0.274	20.87	2.20	22	2.80
Average	8.62	0.091	6.95	0.73	7.3	0.93
Search 3						
File 1	39.47	0.283	19.81	2.26	87	17.40

Source: Made available by Information Systems and Research, Inc., Monroeville, Pennsylvania.

TABLE 5.9 Average Costs and Times for Three Online Searches of the Lockheed System

	Estimated total cost, dollars	Search hours	Cost of file, dollars	Cost of tymnet, dollars	Number of prints	Cost of prints, dollars
Search 1	98.25	0.499	31.06	3.99	393	63.20
Search 2	25.87	0.274	20.87	2.20	22	2.80
Search 3	39.47	0.283	19.81	2.26	87	17.40
Average	54.53	0.352	23.91	2.82	167.3	27.80

Source: Figures made available by Information Systems and Research, Inc., Monroeville, Pennsylvania.

professional rate of $10 an hour for manual searching, this sum of money would make available 7 hrs. or one working day of a professional in a technical library, with $4.53 left over for making photocopies of the applicable references.

WHEN THE USER FINDS THE RESULTS UNSATISFACTORY

The Search Fails to Retrieve a Known Document

While the description (Chap. 3) of using collections of ORed subject terms ANDed into a simple two- or three-way intersection implies that a reasonable amount of hard work with background reference books, thesauri, etc., will produce the desired results, many such searches may fail to yield the single document which is the definitive answer. The client may become aware that the mechanical search has not brought him this valuable document through conversations with his peers, through references in the documents retrieved by the search, or he may see it in a recent journal that comes to his desk. Abstracting services run as much as 6 months behind the appearance of the original document, and, while most present tapes are geared so that mechanical search results will reach the client as quickly as does the hard-copy abstract journal, recently published documents may very well not appear among the search results.

Sometimes, however, a valuable document is on the tape and is not netted by the prepared strategy. This failure is most often traceable to the use of nongeneric terms in indexing a document. A simple example is the general technique of using the names of metals and alloys discussed in the document but not the generic terms METAL or ALLOY. A document about the attack of brass by vinegar may be indexed by BRASS and VINEGAR but not by COPPER ALLOY, ACID, or ACETIC ACID. Such indexing failures cannot help but occur, since the number of indexing terms it is possible to use is limited. A more extensive example appears in Appendix I.

Modifying the Current Awareness Strategy

The descriptions so far made in this chapter have been drawn from experience with "retrospective" or whole-file searching, which can be restricted, of course, in the time period covered. If a strategy, or profile, is applied to the file updates as they appear for the purpose of keeping the client abreast with new developments in the field of interest, the search is referred to as a "current awareness" or SDI (selective dissemination of information) search. When a strategy is used for current awareness searching, it can be continuously evaluated and modified to cover changes in client interest and changes in indexing orientations. Appendix II is a flow diagram for the continuous checking of current awareness strategies. Studies directed toward optimizing the results of current awareness automated searches are reported in [6].

SUMMARY

Two measures of search effectiveness, recall and precision, based on the number of relevant items retrieved and the total number of relevant items in the file, have been developed. Precision, defined as the ratio of relevant items retrieved to the total number of items retrieved, is not an accurate measure of search effectiveness. Recall, while an accurate gauge of search effectiveness, is not measurable for real searches. Costs can undermine search effectiveness. An impression of ineffective searching can result from the system's failure to retrieve a known relevant document. When a search is made repetitively on a current awareness basis the search strategy can be optimized as the results from search after search are studied.

APPENDIX I   Example of Indexing Inaccuracies

For a search on the subject of "lubrication of carbon steel tubing for cold drawing" an article entitled "Bonderizing Assists Cold Drawing of Tubes" came to the attention of the client but was not among the listed results of the mechanical search. Investigation revealed that the document was in the file, which was searchable by index terms only. The index terms for the document, only four in number, were TUBES, COLD DRAWING, BONDERIZING, and METAL WORKING.
　　The search strategy had been

(LUBRICATION + LUBRICANT + COATING + COATINGS) * (COLD

DRAWING + METAL DRAWING + COLD WORKING + METAL

FORMING + TUBEMAKING)

BONDERIZING is a more specific term than either LUBRICATION or COATING and would have been used had the analyst been aware of it. The application of the term BONDERIZING to the file yielded five references not cited from the original strategy. Two of the five references, including the one found by the client, were relevant to the search. The use of a specific index term such as BONDERIZING is a recommended procedure for the indexer because it will permit the searcher to retrieve everything on the specific subject of bonderizing. That the more generic terms LUBRICATION and COATING are not used makes searching difficult for an equally specific search goal such as "lubrication of tube drawing processes."

APPENDIX II A Flow Diagram for Current Awareness

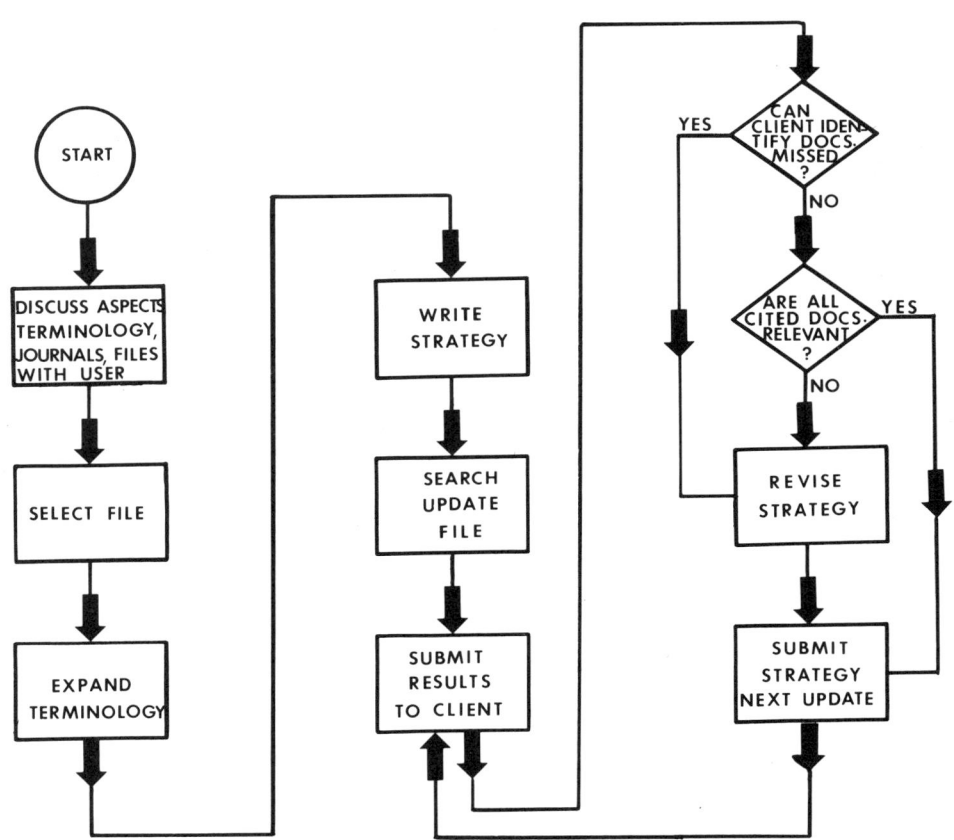

REFERENCES

1. J. W. Perry and Allen Kent. Documentation and Information Retrieval. Interscience, New York, 1957, p. 27.
2. F. H. Barker, D. C. Veal, and B. K. Wyatt. "Retrieval Experiments Based on Chemical Abstracts Condensates." UKCIS Research Report 2, March, 1974. Nottingham, The United Kingdom.
3. F. W. Lancaster. "MEDLARS: Report on the Evaluation of its Operating Efficiency." Amer. Doc. 20(2), 1969, 119.

References

4. F. Wilfrid Lancaster. *Information Retrieval Systems.* Wiley, New York, 1968, p. 56.
5. Stanley A. Elman. "Cost Comparisons of Manual and Online Computerized Literature Searching." *Spec. Libr.* *66*(1), January 1975, 12-18.
6. F. H. Barker, B. K. Wyatt, and D. C. Veal. "Report on the Evaluation of an Experimental Computer-Based Current-Awareness Service for Chemists." *J. Amer. Soc. Inf. Sci.* *23*(2), March-April 1972, 85.

chapter 6
How Computerized Retrieval Works

INTRODUCTION: USÉ OF THE COMPUTER
FOR MECHANIZED RETRIEVAL

Two forms of computers exist: analog and digital. The analog computer processes by electronically converting measurements to voltages and manipulating the representative voltages to calculate the data needed. The digital computer operates by using discrete numbers (digits) to represent identities, and manipulates them by the simple arithmetic functions of addition and subtraction. The digital computer, since it can represent alphabetics by numbers, is used for literature storage and retrieval.

Several capabilities of computers are important in the field of information retrieval. First, computer memory can store and manipulate document identifications by the thousands. Second, the computer can search and identify information at great speed. Third, the computer can store and modify complicated instructions for selecting information. More detailed descriptions of how the computer works will be found in [1-4].

While the original method of searching by computer was to load the searchable file into the computer memory and then to load a program directing how the search should be performed, it is now possible to contact a computer facility directly, "online," and to observe the results of each step in the searching process. The original method allowed several searches to be run at the same time, the results being printed out on an offline printer. When the searcher operates online it is possible to modify the search in process should that become necessary, and to direct the printer to print only what are acceptable search results. Several large companies such as Lockheed and the System Development Corporation supply this service. It is, of course, more expensive to make the individual search, but since the need to process in one's own computer with attendant expenses such as housekeeping tapes and disks is eliminated, the online service often has a direct economic appeal.

HOW INFORMATION IS STORED FOR ELECTRONIC ACCESS

Introduction

In order to process information, a computer must store information in a form which can be read electronically. Storage media can be keypunched cards, film strips, magnetic tape, magnetic disk memory, or the computer's primary memory, which may be core memory, semiconductor memory, or bubble memory. If the information is stored on a deck of keypunched cards, it is read into the computer memory by a card reader before processing takes place. Magnetic tapes or disk packs may be searched directly by the processing computer, and may also be stored when not needed. A large library of tapes and disks is usually an adjunct to any computer-based searching service. Only a relatively small, finite amount of information can be stored permanently in the primary memory of a computer, and the computer cannot be used for other purposes. Since a computer may be used for a variety of tasks, tying up the primary memory with a file of information is usually considered economically unsound at the present state of the art.

Media

When the size of files of information began to grow as a result of the "information explosion," the boxes and drawers of file cards maintained to list references in logical order became too large for easy manipulation. Various forms of notched cards, such as edge-notched, marginal hole, and keysort cards, were developed [2,3,5]. Punched cards code information by means of a punch, or lack of a punch, at specified positions on the card. When random coding of three rows of possible notching around the perimeter of the card is utilized, as in the "Needle/Sort" card (Fig. 6.1), a file of up to 10,000 references can be controlled by author, title words, or any characteristic of the reference that seems important. While such files may seem pedestrian when compared with computer manipulation and results, they are not to be overlooked for small personal files, for which their ease of access and low cost make them quite suitable.

The most common form of punched card used today is the IBM card (Fig. 6.2). The card shown in Fig. 6.2 is the card used to keypunch information for entry into a computer. Figure 6.3 shows a similar card, with only half as many columns, on which the positions are semiperforated so that data may be punched into the card with a pencil tip. Besides being used to enter information into a computer, such cards can be manipulated on a sorter into chosen lists and ordered lists, and the information printed from the cards in the sorted order. An extensive discussion of punched card manipulation is given in [2]. The information is coded on the cards in 80 vertical columns with 12 punching positions in each column. Ten

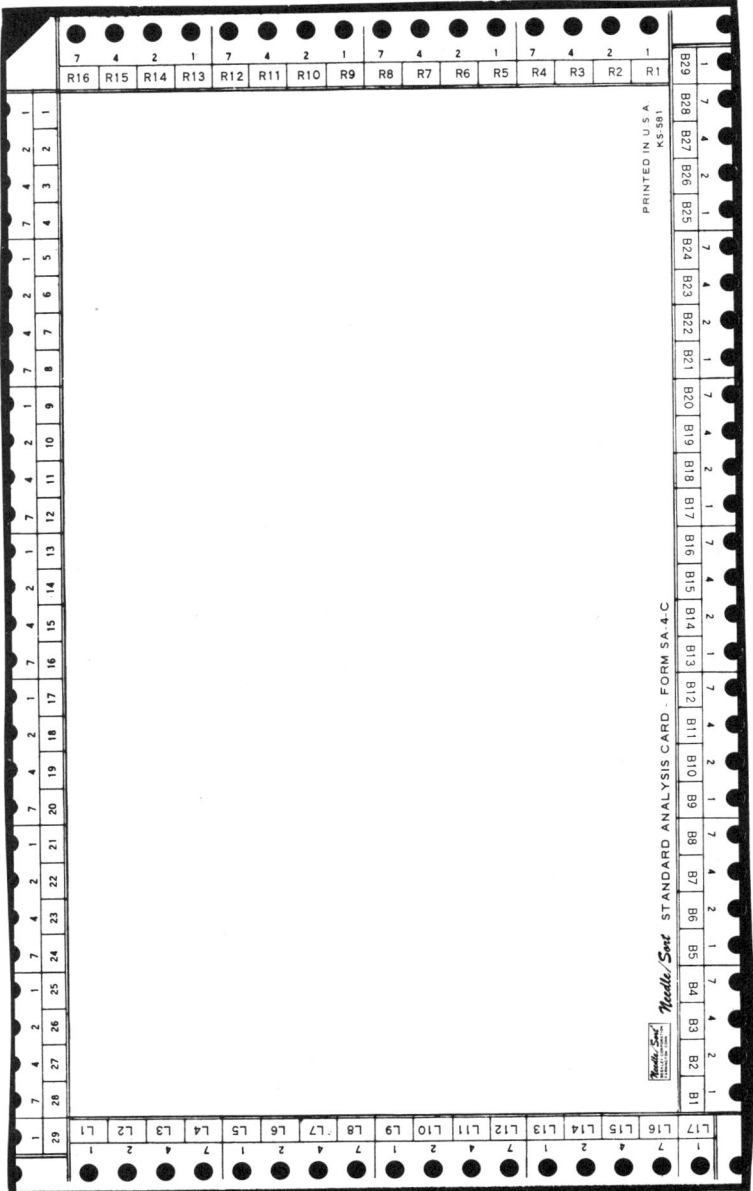

Figure 6.1 Needle/Sort notched card. (Permission for reproduction granted by the Beekley Corporation, Farmington, Connecticut.)

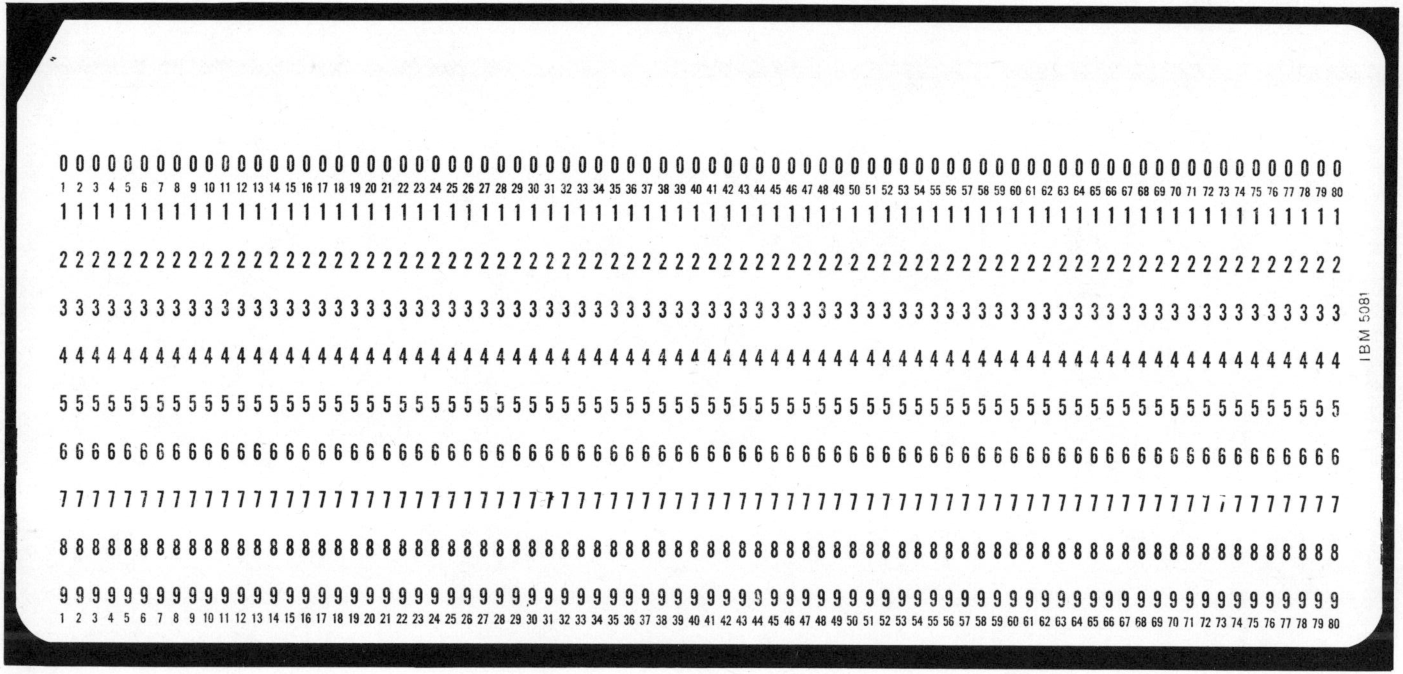

Figure 6.2 IBM Keypunch Card Form 5081. (Reprinted by permission International Business Machines Corporation.)

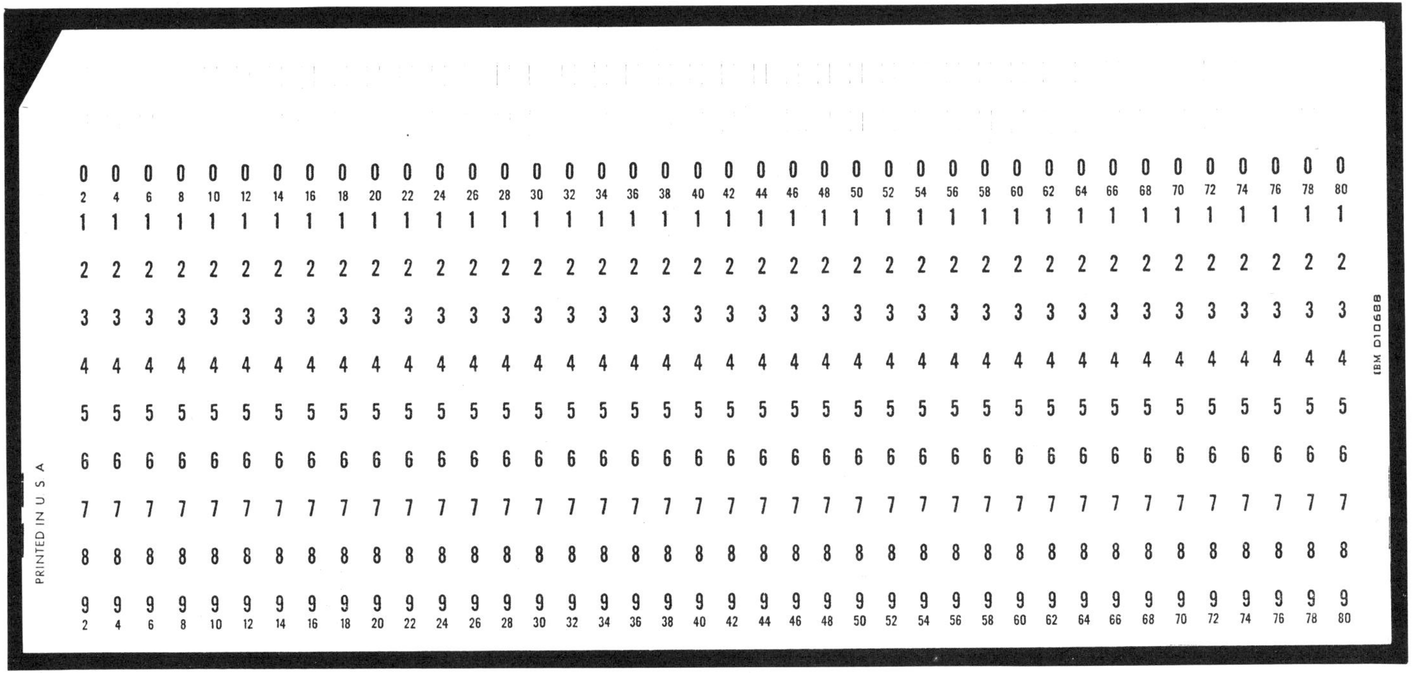

Figure 6.3 IBM D1D6BB card. (Reprinted by permission International Business Machines Corporation.)

punch positions represent the digits 0 to 9. The other two punch positions are control positions. A combination of two punches, one in one of the positions 1 to 9, and the other in one of the two control positions or in the 0 position, represents an alphabetic character [5]. The holes in the cards can be read mechanically by means of pins passing through them, electrically by wire brushes which make contact through the holes, or photoelectrically by using optical sensors. The codes on paper tapes, magnetic tapes, and microcards are similar [2,3,6].

A perforated paper tape can be prepared by keyboard punching to produce a continuous length of coded information [2,3]. Both paper tapes and keypunched cards can be used to store information before it is loaded into computer memory for processing. In this way the computer's primary memory is kept free for other tasks when the computer is not being used for searching. Tapes or cards can also be utilized for entering search strategies for retrieval of information. Preparation of an error-free punched tape will save communication time in the transmittal of information over the teletype machines often used to enter information to remote installations.

Another method of storing information is microphotography. Bibliographic references, references with abstracts, or whole documents can be stored on microfilm, microfiche, film strips, and film inserts. A microfilm recording of a file can be made and stored in cartridge reels, coded so that the frame which the user wishes to view can be selected by keying. An example of such a machine is the Recordak microfilm viewer, which can be used to view records such as Chemical Abstracts. This system makes it possible to save much space that would otherwise go to the storage of journals. Microfiche is another method for storing documents on film. The size of the microfiche film is 105 x 148 mm, with 72 page images on each microfiche. Recently developed has been the ultrafiche, with which 2000 page images are stored on a film strip 1-1/2 x 6 inches in size. A single page image may be stored on an aperture card, the rest of the card being occupied by identifying and sorting information. This information can, of course, be coded by notches, by punches, or by optically sensible dots on the card. Such coded aperture cards can be built into an information retrieval system so that the image page or complete document can be called up on a viewer or cathode ray tube for examination [3]. An extensive discussion of document storage and retrieval from microimages will be found in [6-8].

Modern computers function by storing information magnetically. An array of magnetic "bits"—in the form of iron doughnuts in the computer core or of areas (bubbles) on a magnetizable ribbon or disk—are made magnetic or nonmagnetic by the application of a small electric current. The array then consists of an arrangement of "yesses" and "nos" comparable to the holes in keypunched cards or paper tape.

Magnetic tape is advantageous for information storage since it is inexpensive, can store large volumes of data, and is available for mounting on the computer at any time. Information on the tape is arranged in some kind of sequential order—by accession number, alphabetically by the author's name, or in whatever order is most convenient for the producers of the tape. Ordering by accession number is most usual because new material can be added as it is acquired to the end of the tape, instead of being inserted in the middle, which necessitates rewriting all the subsequent information on the tape.

It should be mentioned that problems can occur with the use of tapes as well as with card decks. Tapes can be misplaced, get scratched, or become magnetically contaminated if not used. Duplicate backup tapes are always good insurance. It can also happen that there are flaws on the tapes and a recorded surrogate may not appear on the final tape. Maintaining a good tape library involves considerable work—checking tapes, cleaning tapes, recording tapes, etc.

Magnetic disks differ from magnetic tapes in that document records may be randomly accessed, whereas magnetic tapes must be processed sequentially from the beginning until the required address is found. Information on a disk is magnetically coded into the circular bands called tracks across the disk, and the read or write head may move to any address specified.

Codes

Information is stored in the selected media as a digital code. To enable the information processing to take place without examining the full content of each bibliographic entry or record, the surrogates for the items are either placed in fixed positions or fields, or a directory is included with each record that points to the location of each field within the coded item. For instance, for keypunched cards, columns 1 through 7 may be reserved for the unique item number, columns 8 through 62 for the authors' names, 63 through 80 for the journal CODEN, volume, and year, and columns 1 through 80 on the second card for index terms. Since some information files have titles and even abstracts to store as well as index terms, maintaining a file of any size on keypunched cards to be read into the computer each time a search is made is very unwieldy. Even the entry of the query words to be matched by the search in the form of keypunched cards involves so many maintenance problems with the card decks that usually, if the searching is performed as a batch process, a magnetic tape is prepared of the search strategies. When searching takes place in interactive or online mode, the strategy is read into temporary memory. If it will be used more than once it can be stored in a long-term memory and deleted when it is no longer useful.

The basic code for computer manipulation is the binary code, which consists of numbers built on the base 2 rather than on the base 10 used for common arithmetic. The numeral 110 to the base 10 stands for one hundred and ten individual items, while to the base 2 is represents six items. Since

Information Storage for Electronic Access   113

the fundamental structure of the computer is the on-off magnetic field in
each position, the binary code is an easy way to represent information,
since each digit is a 1 or a 0. Each digit is referred to as a bit (binary
digit).
   Two coding systems using binary bits for information retrieval are
recognized: the ASCII and the EBCDIC. These systems both use 8 bits to
represent a character: 7 data bits and one parity bit. For example, the
character "A" might have the pattern 11000001 in ASCII, and 00100001 in
EBCDIC. It is essential that the stored information be coded in the same
form in which the program for searching is keyed. ASCII has been developed as a standard, and while EBCDIC systems are numerous, so that
Chemical Abstracts, for instance, prepares its tapes in both forms, ASCII
is the standard format recognized by The American National Standards
Institute [9].

What is Stored

In the preparation of bibliographic files the complete entry for an item is
usually referred to as a record, and the searchable subsets of the record,
i.e., the parts of the item which have predetermined positions in the record,
are called fields. A fixed field allots a set space to that part of the item.
If the documents are stored in fixed fields there may be a character limitation to every surrogate which is used as an entry point. For instance,
index terms may be limited to twenty characters. If this is true then a
request to search a term of more than twenty characters will result in an
"error" message, or in an automatic truncation. As a result, most bibliographic records use a variable field length approach. A lucid and detailed
description of storage of information for electronic handling is contained
in [4].
   The surrogates which may be used to identify a document include the
title; the authors; cited reference authors; journal, year, volume, and page;
the authors' affiliations and geographic locations; the language of the document; index terms or keywords, both major and minor; an abstract; relevant numerical data; and a unique document accession number. Sometimes
the entire document, for example a news item, is stored. While any term
in the item can be a document surrogate "stand-in," only those terms that
the searching program will accept as entry points can be used in searching.
Not all possible surrogates are stored for every file. A restricted file may
store only the index terms and the accession numbers. Even though a file
is very comprehensive in surrogate coverage, its searchability still depends
on the search program. A stored abstract does not mean a searched abstract unless the program is written to search abstracts as well as keywords
and other surrogates.

File Organization

To permit searching, the file of information must be organized in such a manner that search patterns can be iterated successively in the same way over each stored item. That is, each item of the file must have the same recognizable pattern as each other item. Each item of a bibliographic file may contain such identifiable parts as title, authors, journal, language, descriptors, and abstracts. An example of a series of items from one file is shown in Fig. 6.4. For the ordinary bibliographic citation, the identifiable parts usually consist of alphabetic words, but may include numeric data (besides journal number and date) such as temperatures, pressures, percentage compositions, strengths, wavelengths, and the like. In chemical literature it is also possible to represent structures, for example by Wiswesser line formulas and registry numbers. In order to make retrieval easy, and to provide a short, quick method of identifying each item, a unique number (abstract number) is part of the item. This number if issued as the item is entered into the file, usually in chronological serial order. There may or may not be a stored file in which each item is entered in serial order by item number as shown in Fig. 6.4. The items may be stored in lists, for example by author, by journal, or by index term. The file may consist of only one such list, or there may be several separate

item #	28100
title	STAINLESS STEEL MELTING BY TWO LOW COST PROCESSES.
authors	CARLSON, R. F.; SHAW, R. B.;
jr. ref.	IRON AND STEEL ENG v 49, n 8, Aug. 1972, p. 53-65
auth aff	BRACKENRIDGE WORKS, ALLEGHENY LUDLUM STEEL CORP, PA
descrip	METAL MELTING; FURNACES; MELTING; STAINLESS STEEL; FURNACES, ELECTRIC;
item #	32611
title	COST FACTORS IN FORGING STAINLESS STEEL AND HIGH TEMPERATURE ALLOYS
authors	WALSH, A. M.;
jr. ref.	PRECIS METAL v 31, n 2, Feb. 1973, p. 26-28
auth aff	HIGH TEMPERATURE ALLOYS CARPENTER TECHNOLOGY CORP
descrip	FORGING; STAINLESS STEEL; METALS AND ALLOYS; METAL FORMING;
item #	47101
title	DECARBURIZATION OF STAINLESS STEEL 2. A MATHEMATICAL MODEL AND A PROCESS OPTIMIZATION FOR INDUSTRIAL SCAIE SYSTEMS
authors	SZEKELEY, J.; ASAI, S.;
jr. ref.	METALL. TRANS. v 5, n 7, Jul 1974, p. 1573-1580
auth aff	STATE UNIV. OF NY BUFFALO
descrip	STEELMAKING; ELECTRIC FURNACE PROCESS; STAINLESS STEEL; MATHEMATICAL MODELS; COST ACCOUNTING;

Figure 6.4 Item records entered into file as accessioned chronologically, and serial accession numbers issued.

Information Storage for Electronic Access   115

lists, each containing all the file items. The index term lists may resemble library cataloging in that the item is placed under one or more general categories (Fig. 6.5). Alternatively, the item may be identified in inverted

ELECTRIC FURNACE STEELMAKING
item #   28100
title   STAINLESS STEEL MELTING BY TWO LOW COST PROCESSES.
authors   CARLSON, R. F.; SHAW, R. B.;
jr. ref. IRON AND STEEL ENG v 49, n 8, Aug. 1972, p. 53-65
auth aff BRACKENRIDGE WORKS, ALLEGHENY LUDLUM STEEL CORP, PA
descrip   METAL MELTING; FURNACES; MELTING; STAINLESS STEEL;
          FURNACES, ELECTRIC;
item #   47101
title   DECARBURIZATION OF STAINLESS STEEL 2. A MATHEMAT-
          ICAL MODEL AND A PROCESS OPTIMIZATION FOR INDUS-
          TRIAL SCALE SYSTEMS
authors   SZEKELEY, J.; ASAI, S.;
jr. ref. METALL. TRANS. v 5, n 7, Jul 1974, p. 1573-1580
auth aff STATE UNIV. OF NY BUFFALO
descrip   STEELMAKING; ELECTRIC FURNACE PROCESS; STAINLESS
          STEEL; MATHEMATICAL MODELS; COST ACCOUNTING;
MATHEMATICAL MODELS
item #   47101
title   DECARBURIZATION OF STAINLESS STEEL 2. A MATHEMAT-
          ICAL MODEL AND A PROCESS OPTIMIZATION FOR INDUS-
          TRIAL SCALE SYSTEMS
authors   SZEKELEY, J.; ASAI, S.;
jr. ref. METALL. TRANS. v 5, n 7, Jul 1974, p. 1573-1580
auth aff STATE UNIV. OF NY BUFFALO
descrip   STEELMAKING; ELECTRIC FURNACE PROCESS; STAINLESS
          STEEL; MATHEMATICAL MODELS; COST ACCOUNTING;
STAINLESS STEEL
item #   28100
title   STAINLESS STEEL MELTING BY TWO LOW COST PROCESSES.
authors   CARLSON, R. F.; SHAW, R. B.;
jr. ref. IRON AND STEEL ENG v 49, n 8, Aug. 1972, p. 53-65
auth aff BRACKENRIDGE WORKS, ALLEGHENY LUDLUM STEEL CORP, PA
descrip   METAL MELTING; FURNACES; MELTING; STAINLESS STEEL;
          FURNACES, ELECTRIC;
item #   32611
title   COST FACTORS IN FORGING STAINLESS STEEL AND HIGH
          TEMPERATURE ALLOYS
authors   WALSH, A. M.;
jr. ref. PRECIS METAL v 31, n 2, Feb. 1973, p. 26-28
auth aff HIGH TEMPERATURE ALLOYS CARPENTER TECHNOLOGY CORP
descrip   FORGING; STAINLESS STEEL; METALS AND ALLOYS; METAL
          FORMING;
item #   47101
title   DECARBURIZATION OF STAINLESS STEEL 2. A MATHEMAT-
          ICAL MODEL AND A PROCESS OPTIMIZATION FOR INDUS-
          TRIAL SCALE SYSTEMS
authors   SZEKELEY, J.; ASAI, S.;
jr. ref. METALL. TRANS. v 5, n 7, Jul 1974, p. 1573-1580
auth aff STATE UNIV. OF NY BUFFALO
descrip   STEELMAKING; ELECTRIC FURNACE PROCESS; STAINLESS
          STEEL; MATHEMATICAL MODELS; COST ACCOUNTING;

Figure 6.5 File in which items are stored by category although issued unique item numbers as they are acquired.

file fashion, that is, listed in the subfiles of which the item is a member—author, journal, term, etc. (Fig. 6.6). In any case the items themselves may be separately stored in sequential order by item number, as is necessary if the original storage medium is matnetic tape. Or the items may be stored on a direct-access device, for example a disk, but still retrievable by item number.

Figure 6.6 was put together using index terms and meaningful title words from the items in Fig. 6.4. A real free-text inverted file would include author names, journal names, and author affiliations, as well as words from the title, index terms and words from index terms, and other data elements. It may also include words from an abstract. It is obvious from this example why nonrelevant citations (false drops) occur so frequently in a mechanized system. For instance, from Fig. 6.6, it is seen that the request combination STEEL and SCALE would yield item 47101, which has nothing whatever to do with the formation of scale on steel. Item 28100 would be of only marginal interest to a user interested in a study of costs involved in stainless steel processing.

ALLOYS	32611;		
COST	28100;	32611;	
COST ACCOUNTING	47101;		
DECARBURIZATION	47101;		
ELECTRIC FURNACE PROCESS	47101;		
FACTORS	32611;		
FORGING	32611;		
FURNACES	28100;		
FURNACES, ELECTRIC	28100;		
HIGH	32611;		
INDUSTRIAL	47101;		
LOW	28100;		
MATHEMATICAL	47101;		
MATHEMATICAL MODELS	47101;		
MELTING	28100;		
METAL FORMING	32611;		
METAL MELTING	28100;		
METALS AND ALLOYS	32611;		
MODEL	47101;		
OPTIMIZATION	47101;		
PROCESS	47101;		
PROCESSES	28100;		
SCALE	47101;		
STAINLESS	28100;	32611;	47101;
STAINLESS STEEL	28100;	32611;	47101;
STEEL	28100;	32611;	47101;
STEELMAKING	47101;		
SYSTEMS	47101;		
TEMPERATURE	32611;		
TWO	28100;		

Figure 6.6 Inverted file. Item numbers stored under applicable terms. Used in conjunction with file such as that of Fig. 6.4 when a bibliographic printout is requested.

Information Storage for Electronic Access

To make good use of available storage space, the usual process is to store as inverted files. The terms may also be hashcoded, that is, fixed-length numeric codes may be substituted for alphabetic terms in order to facilitate storage. A combination of hashcoding and an inverted list is often used in online systems.

When information is stored year after year, forming a large tape library, retrospective searching—searching back in time—becomes difficult. Usually the back file will be broken up into years. Sometimes it is wise to break up the back file into subsets so that an entire year of items need not be searched but only the applicable parts. There are many ways in which this can be done. Separating into months would make it easy to retrieve a particular item if its date were known, but such requests are rare in technical searches. For a file such as the New York Times Information Bank, separation by smaller time segments than years is useful.

An extremely valuable approach for the back files of Chemical Condensates has been to separate them by the large subject section groups of Chemical Abstracts. These section groups are Organic, Biochemistry, Macromolecular, Chemical Engineering, and Physical and Analytical. Subject overlap does occur but it was found [10] that two or at most three sections will give an adequate search, thus cutting the cost of searching by at least 2/5.

Another way a file can be broken down into smaller subsets is by separating books and monographs from journal and magazine articles.

Reference Material

At the same time that the file is built with an inverted hashcoded structure, it is necessary to form reference dictionaries so that the searcher can know what terms are available and what related terms exist. These reference materials are available online for online files and are usually kept updated. Printed or microfiche issues of the reference files are also usually available, but these, of course, cannot be as up to date as the online reference material. They do provide an easily accessible reference for use in planning a strategy, and it saves time to use them and then to update online if necessary. Examples of such printed reference dictionaries are Lockheed's DIALIST [11] and Engineering Index's SHE [12].

Batch Versus Online

While the inverted file or an indexed file is practically essential for the efficient operation of an online search system, the batch process, because it processes several searches at the same time, can use a sequential file without too much loss of time or storage space. Many small files used in-house are set up in this way and operate well. Although efficiency might be increased by converting to the inverted-file, hashcoded, or some other indexing access method, the cost of conversion, including the necessary checking, loss of time, and dictionary preparation, would be prohibitive.

An example of the development of a fact retrieval system is given in reference [13].

HOW INFORMATION IS RETRIEVED

Punched Cards

The information on punched cards of the 80-column variety can be retrieved by reading them into computer memory and searching by a computer program. They can also be sorted on a mechanical sorter [5]. Edge-notched cards can be needle sorted. Accurate searches of a limited subject field can be performed on personal files of the needle-sort variety if they are precisely indexed.

Computerized Information Systems

A computer-based information system consists of procedures for reading the searchable information into memory, the development of a suitable command language to tell the computer how to perform the search in the logical pattern required by the searcher, and the preparation of or access to reference dictionaries needed by the searcher in order to select terms that are used in the system. The logical requirements consist of procedures for examining each record in the file for the presence of one of a list of specified terms (the OR relationship), or the presence of a group of specified terms (the AND relationship), or the nonappearance of a specified term (the NOT relationship). In addition, the system may have the capability of finding phrases or strings of terms, or of identifying all terms beginning with a specified group of letters (right truncation) or ending with a group of letters (left truncation) or having a group of letters within the term.

The capability of limiting the search to only a portion of the file is easily achieved in computerized searching. If the search is for papers by a certain author, the computer can be instructed to search only the fields containing author names. If the author's name, the year of publication, and the journal are known the search can be narrowed by searching for the coincidence of the pertinent data between author, year of publication, and journal identification fields. The most common limit used in present-day searching is of the years covered. For example, the user may be interested only in items published since 1974 even though the file goes back to 1969. Such a search is frequently made on the basis of accession numbers rather than of the year of publication. The computer is requested to limit the search to items whose accession numbers are between that of the first item of 1974 and that of the latest date. Some programs, such as the Lockheed DIALOG program, permit a "nine fill" to be used as the upper limit, i.e., to use an accession number consisting of all 9's, so that it is unnecessary to ascertain what the latest accession number for the file is.

An easily achieved spinoff of a computer-based search system is a listing of all searchable terms in alphabetical order so that spelling can be checked. These dictionaries appear in hard copy [14], on microfiche [11], or online. Most such dictionaries are cross-referenced to give related terms. The depth and quality of cross referencing varies from file to file.

More than 100 different search systems have been developed to deal with the mechanical retrieval of information. All of them claim to have features different from and more efficient than those of other systems. Some of the systems are general data management systems which extract numerical data and give the user tables and diagrams. Most have been developed specifically to list bibliographic references. Examples of search systems are PIRETS [15], ORBIT [16], DIALOG [17], STAIRS [18], and SMART [19].

The selection of the search system, from the point of view of the user, hinges on the availability of searching capabilities such as the following:

1. Controlled vocabulary, that is, a restricted list of acceptable index terms which can be used with confidence by the searcher. For instance, the term "alloy" in a controlled vocabulary system could be the surrogate for documents discussing one alloy or several, the process of alloying, and special alloys such as brass or pewter.
2. Hierarchical searching, which lists for the searcher all documents with subgeneric terms when the generic term is requested. The search term "metal" would uncover articles about individual metals such as silver or vanadium as well as articles which discuss metals in general.
3. Free-text searching, which permits the searcher to anticipate the appearance of a definitive word, not necessarily an index term, in the title or abstract. For instance, one might reasonably search for articles containing "UFO" in the title.
4. Subheading searching, which permits the use as a single search term of the heading-subheading relationship. For instance, in the Engineering Index COMPENDEX system, CORROSION/ELECTRO-CHEMICAL can be searched for all entries under the heading Corrosion, subheading Electrochemical. If the relationship CORROSION AND ELECTROCHEMICAL were searched the listing would be different, including all items which have "corrosion" and "electrochemical" as index terms.
5. Alphanumeric Code Searching, where codes have been prepared for primary subjects of interest.

6. Word stem searching, by which all occurrences of words containing the designated word stem can be found. For instance, -METHYLENE would retrieve hexamethylene dichloride, HEXAMETHYL- would retrieve hexamethylene and hexamethyldiethyl toluene, and -METHYL- would retrieve hexamethylene, hexamethyldiethyl, and many other organic chemicals.
7. Searching of phrases or strings of terms: the ability to differentiate between phrases such as "the management of information" and "management information" is of great value.
8. Postings of the number of documents in the system for any requested term.
9. Postings for combinations of terms.
10. Boolean logic, using the Boolean connectors OR, AND, and NOT as links among combinations of terms.
11. The connectors "greater than" and "less than."
12. "Nesting" of Boolean logic: the ability to search, for instance, COPPER or ZINC linked with ALLOY, in addition to the term BRASS, in relation to MELTING.
13. The ability to store and recall a successful strategy for use on another file, or a future file update.
14. The ability to limit the search by portion of the file or by date of publication.
15. The ability to rank the output by some criterion such as specificity of terms.
16. The ability to modify the strategy by feedback from items identified as relevant.
17. The ability to combine data bases and search as a unit.
18. Batch-mode searching, that is, the entry of a group of strategies to be searched in one operation.
19. The application of the system to the interactive mode so that on-line search is possible.
20. The elimination from the listed results of duplicate references located by different search terms or combinations of terms, so that each reference appears only once.
21. Selection of printout format.

When selecting the search system, the efficiency with which the results are achieved is of importance because of time, cost, and storage factors. While all of the above capabilities are desirable, some must be foregone because of limitations in storage space. Free-text searching is both desirable and expensive in terms of computer processing time. So valuable is it that it is part of systems such as DIALOG, PIRETS, and ORBIT. Hierarchical searching is a vital subroutine to many searches. For instance, it might be almost impossible to have all metallic index terms covered when the search is for all metals without either such a subroutine or else controlled indexing which always indexes to generically related terms. Left truncation is an expensive computer process, but invaluable for chemical searching. It is available in the PIRETS program. Phrase searching is performed by connectors which specify how many words may intervene between keywords and whether the keywords must occur in a given order. It is available in most search systems, including ORBIT, DIALOG, and PIRETS. Most systems provide postings of terms and combinations of terms. Most systems are based on Boolean logic, although weighting of terms may be included to permit ranking, as in STAIRS.

Use of the connectors "greater than" and "less than" can be a valuable capability in searching technical files but is not available for most systems. Nesting of logic can be achieved for most search systems. Some require the listing of a series of operations, while for others the operation can be achieved in a single statement.

Limiting, particularly by time covered, is available for most systems. Modification of a strategy by feedback of relevant items is not commonly offered on commercial data bases. SMART is a system for which it is possible. Combination of data bases so that repetition of references is eliminated would be a most useful adjunct to commercial online systems. To make it possible, however, would require standardization and detailed reformatting of the data bases by the organizations offering online searching.

How to Access a Computerized File

<u>Processing</u>. The fundamental process in searching an organized file is to apply to the file search terms that are related in such a way that the logic paraphrases the query. The preparation of a search pattern or strategy is discussed at length in Chap. 3. When a search is instituted, the abstract numbers for the operable terms are compared according to the logic relationships. The abstract numbers are put in temporary memory and at the end of the search a complete list of the identified abstracts are printed out. Duplicate references are eliminated by a program subroutine.

<u>Organizations Selling Mechanical Searches.</u> Mechanical searches of literature may be purchased from five different types of source: retrieval service centers; data centers; brokers; online services; and libraries, through networking. It is possible to purchase tapes or disks of information from suppliers to process in your own computer.

Retrieval Service Centers: To make the contents of organized mechanical files, particularly government files, available to the public, searches are sold at a nominal cost by various retrieval service centers throughout the United States. Most of these service centers are academically based and more or less subsidized by the federal or state government. Examples are the National Aeronautics and Space Administration Industrial Applications Centers such as KASC (at the University of Pittsburgh), NERAC (at the University of Connecticut), STRC (at the University of North Carolina) and WESRAC (at the University of Southern California). Other retrieval centers are at the University of Georgia, the University of Illinois, and the State University of New York. Among privately owned and operated retrieval centers are Dow-Jones of New York and the Institute for Scientific Information in Philadelphia, which also sells tapes to the Lockheed and SDC online services.

Data Centers: Another kind of information-supplying organization is the data center, which will provide numeric information upon the user's request. Examples of such organizations are the Thermophysical Properties Center at Purdue University; the Alloy Data Center, Metallurgy Division, the National Bureau of Standards; and the Superconductive Materials Data Center, General Electric Company, Research and Development Center.

Brokers: A new profession has emerged in the last 5 years, that of the information broker. The information broker is a specialist who knows where to purchase searches to meet the requirements of his clients. He may be a user of online services such as Lockheed or SDC through his own terminal; he may have contacts with various retrieval centers; and usually he is able to make use of a nearby technical library. The broker is an expert in interviewing the user and uncovering what will satisfy the user's needs, in knowing what files will provide the required answers, in knowing where to access the files, and in setting up logical search strategies.

Online Retrieval: It is now possible to access online some of the largest retrieval centers in the world. Examples are Lockheed and SDC in California and BRS in New York. A comparison of the two online systems Lockheed and SDC [20] demonstrated that it is wise to use all available online systems that have files of potential value in an area of interest. Since no fees need to be paid except upon use, the searcher should be knowledgeable about and have a chargeable identification number for those online services which are needed. The choice of a terminal, which can be rented by the month or purchased, is important, and the subject is thoroughly discussed in [21]. Contact with the service may be by direct wire or by special communications network such as TELENET or TYMNET. Charges will be made depending on the length of time of the connection. It is necessary in the interactive online mode for the user to be able to communicate with the computer. He needs to be trained for the system at workshops held by the services he is using.

Library Networking: The concept of library networking was introduced for the purpose of making the large holdings of a number of libraries available to the users of all of them. Two approaches to such a network are possible. On the one hand, the user may know what book or journal he is looking for, in other words, he may already have identified the relevant document. In this case the user wants to know where he must go to read the volume, whether he may borrow it, and whether, within copyright restrictions, he may obtain copies of the interesting pages. On the other hand, the user may not have identified the relevant documents and may want to have an information retrieval search made in the networked libraries. This of course requires a search tape. The tape could be entered by author. The search strategy might be a request for all listed publications by the named authors; or the tape could be entered by journal. The inquiry would be about the availability of the required journals. Alternatively, the user might present a subject which might be for as small a classification as possible, or might cover a range of LC numbers, or, if the tape permitted, might be a large information search incorporating all the major terms from titles and descriptors. Discussions of the field of library networking will be found in [22, 23].

SUMMARY

Published information is stored for computerized retrieval in the form of punched cards, punched tape, magnetic tape, magnetic disk, or magnetic core. It is stored in a coded form. The way the information is organized depends on the surrogates made available by the file. The information is retrieved by matching what is in the file with what is requested by the search program. Searches for published information may be obtained from retrieval service centers, data centers, brokers, online service suppliers, and library networking.

REFERENCES

1. G. Salton. "Information Storage and Retrieval." Sc. Report #ISR-7 to the National Science Foundation, The Computation Laboratory of Harvard University, Cambridge, Massachusetts, June 1964.
2. Allen Kent. Textbook on Mechanized Information Retrieval. Wiley-Interscience, New York, 1962.
3. Joseph Becker and R. M. Hayes. Information Storage and Retrieval. Wiley, New York, 1964.
4. Charles T. Meadow. Man-Machine Communication. Wiley-Interscience, New York, 1970.
5. Jack Belzer. "Punched Card System." Libr. Sci. 2(1), March 1965, p. 69.
6. Margaret C. Kolb. "Document Storage and Handling in Information Systems." In Technical Information Center Administration (Arthur W. Elias, Ed.). Spartan Books, Washington, D.C., 1965.
7. B. J. S. Williams. "Miniaturized Communications: A Review of Microforms." Libr. Assoc. London, 1970.

8. R. Wicker, R. Neperud, and A. Teplitz. "Microfiche Storage and Retrieval System Study: Final Report." AD 710 000, System Development Corp., Falls Church, Virginia, 1970.
9. Peter B. Schipma. "Generation and Uses of Machine Readable Data Bases." Annu. Rev. Inf. Sci. Technol. 10, 1975, p. 237.
10. Bahaa El Hadidy. "Approaches to the Economical Retrospective Machine-Searching of CA Condensates." ASIS Mid-year Conference, Dayton, Ohio. 1972.
11. "DIALIST" Lockheed Information Systems, Palo Alto, California.
12. Engineering Index, Inc. Subject Headings for Engineering - SHE, 1972 edition. Supplement to 1972 SHE, 1977. Subheading Index 1977. Available from EI, United Engineering Center, New York.
13. Charles H. Kellog. "An Approach to the Online Interrogation of Structural Files of Facts Using Natural Language." AD 661 966. Defense Documentation Center, U. S. Department of Commerce, April 2, 1966.
14. "NASA Thesaurus Alphabetical Update." NASA-SP-7050. NASA Technology Utilization Office, Washington, D. C., 1978.
15. PIRETS Users Handbook. The University of Pittsburgh Bookstore, Pittsburgh, Pennsylvania, 1978.
16. ORBIT Quick Reference Guide. System Development Corporation, Santa Monica, California.
17. A Brief Guide to DIALOG Searching. Lockheed Information Systems, Palo Alto, California.
18. "IBM System 360 and System 370 (OS) Storage and Information Retrieval System." General Information Program Product 5734-XR3. IBM, Germany, Stuttgart, Germany, 1971.
19. G. Salton. "The Evaluation of Automatic Retrieval Procedures - Selected Test Results Using the SMART System." Amer. Doc. 16(3), July 1965, p. 209.
20. Barbara E. Burroughs and Joey Skaff. "Maximizing Online Use on a Single System—Will It Really Save Big Money?" Online 2(2), April 1978, p. 55.
21. Mark S. Radwin. "The Intelligent Person's Guide to Choosing a Terminal for Online Interactive Use." Online 1(1), January 1977, p. 11; 1(2), April 1977, p. 61.
22. F. G. Kilgour and H. D. Davis. "The Development of a Computerized Regional Library System. Final Report." Ohio College Library Center, Columbus, Ohio, 1973, 58 pp.
23. Allen Kent, Thomas J. Galvin, Lee G. Burchinal, Miriam A. Drake, Paul E. Peters, Elaine Caruso, et al. Proceedings. Online Revolution in Libraries, November 14-16, 1977. Marcel Dekker, Inc., 1978.

Glossary

ABI INFORM   A division of Data Courier, Inc. Producer of computer searchable business file INFORM.
ABSTRACT   A condensation of the key elements in a document. It should indicate the purpose of the document, the steps taken to achieve that purpose, and the conclusions reached. Usually not more than 200 words in length.
ABSTRACT JOURNAL   A published journal, appearing at specified time intervals, containing abstracts of recently published primary documents in the subject field of the abstracting service publishing the journal.
ABSTRACT NUMBER   The number assigned to an abstract in an abstract journal to give it an unique identification.
ACCESSION NUMBER   The number assigned to an item entered into an information file, indicating the order of its entry.
ACCESS POINT   The part of a file item which is used to identify it for a given information query.
ADJ   Alphabetic code used in some search programs: indicates that the two words connected by "ADJ" should occur next to each other and in the order specified for a search "hit."
ALGORITHM   A special procedure for solving a logical or mathematical task.
ALPHANUMERIC   A code using both letters and numbers.
ANALOG COMPUTER   A computer in which numbers are converted into measurable quantities, such as lengths or voltages, that can be combined to perform the necessary arithmetic operations.
AND   A Boolean connector indicating that all terms so connected must be present for a search "hit."
ANNOTATED BIBLIOGRAPHY   A bibliography in which notes or comments have been added to individual items.
APERTURE CARD   A punched file card with an opening into which a frame or frames of microfilm have been mounted.
APILIT   Computer searchable data base produced by the American Petroleum Institute. Full name: Index to American Petroleum Institute Abstracts of Refining Literature.

Glossary

ASCII CODE   Standard set of bit combinations used to represent the various alphanumeric characters. ASCII stands for American Standard Code for Information Interchange.

ASIS   American Society for Information Science.

AUTHOR AFFILIATION   The company or institution by which the author is employed.

BATCH PROCESSING   The entry of a number of information-seeking requests into the computer at the same time so that output is received from all the requests without any interference from the operator.

BIBLIOGRAPHIC CITATION   The complete identification of the article, book, report, or other document. Includes title, authors, journal or publisher, pages, and date.

BIBLIOGRAPHIC FILE   A complete list of references to articles, books, reports, or documents; may serve as the base for an information retrieval system.

BIBLIOGRAPHIC REFERENCE   (See Bibliographic Citation.)

BIBLIOGRAPHY   A list of documents related to a subject, author, or other unifying concept.

BIBLIO-PROFILE   A background resumé followed by a comprehensive bibliography. (See Ref. 8 in Chap. 4.)

BINARY CODE   Representation of information using only two symbols, 0 and 1, by writing numbers with the base 2.

BIOSIS   Biosciences Information Service, the producers of the BIOSIS Previews file.

BIT   A contraction of the term "binary digit." The basic unit used to represent information in a binary system.

BOOLEAN LOGIC   The algebra of relating terms by using the concept of linking subsets representing several classes of subsets by the connectors AND (logical product), OR (logical sum), and NOT (logical difference).

BRS   Bibliographic Retrieval Services, Inc. 702 Corporation Park, Scotia, New York 12302. An online retrieval service.

BYTE   A unit of information equal to 8 bits, representing the smallest addressable unit within a memory.

CA   The Chemical Abstracts Service, or its journal Chemical Abstracts.

CACON   CA Condensates. Tape for mechanically searching Chemical Abstracts, produced by the Chemical Abstracts Service. Now superseded by CA Search, which combines the indexing policies of CACON and CASIA.

CARD INDEX   Cards of information arranged in alphabetical or numerical order to serve as an index.

CARD READER   Device to extract information from a card which may be punched, notched, or have magnetic dots.

CASIA   Chemical Abstracts Subject Index Alert. A document-oriented file in CA abstract number sequence with all Volume Index entries for a single abstract.

CA SEARCH   File produced by Chemical Abstracts Service which includes index terms from the Volume Index entries, as well as the issue indexing, for each numerically sequenced abstract number. Registry numbers are included among the surrogates. As a product of Chemical Abstract Service, CA SEARCH replaces CA Condensates and CASIA.

CATEGORIZED BIBLIOGRAPHY   Bibliography in which the entries are listed under appropriate categories of the overall subject.

CBCC CODE 22   The Chemical-Biological Coordination Center Code 22, developed to permit searching by chemical structure. (See Ref. 14 in Chap. 3.)

CHEMICAL STRUCTURE   Interrelation of the chemical elements within a chemical molecule of a compound.

CITATION   (See Bibliographic Citation.)

CITATION INDEX   List of the references mentioned in a document or group of documents. It can be used to find related papers.

CITED REFERENCE   A reference to another document cited in a published paper, report, or monograph.

CLOSED COORDINATED INDEX   An index prepared on the basis of a fixed list of terms (to which new terms are not added) which coordinates possible synonyms to the closed list.

CLOSED INDEXING   Indexing to a closed set of indexing terms.

CODE   A system of symbols or signals for representing information for the purpose of achieving abbreviation or ease of handling.

CODEN   A six-character notation produced and updated by Chemical Abstracts Service to represent the titles of periodicals. An outgrowth of the five-letter notation developed by the American Society for Testing and Materials.

COMMAND LANGUAGE   Job control language for a particular system.

COMPENDEX   Computerized Engineering Index, file produced by Engineering Index, Inc.

COMPUTER   An electronic machine for calculating and for carrying out transformations on information.

COMPUTER MEMORY   The component of a computer designed to store data or instructions so that they may be accessed for processing.

CONDENSATES   (See Cacon.)

CONNECTIVITY TABLES   A method of identifying a chemical compound by its structure (See Ref. 11 in Chap. 3.)

CONNECTORS   The Boolean operators AND, OR, and NOT. Other operators such as ADJ (adjacent), W (with), and F (in the same field) may be used by different search programs.

CONTROLLED INDEXING   Indexing by an authority list or a closed set of index terms.

CONTROLLED VOCABULARY   Authorized vocabulary used for controlled indexing.

COORDINATED INDEX   Index using a controlled vocabulary with "see." (See also Reference.)

CORPORATE SOURCE   The company, corporation, or institution, which an author represents when he publishes a paper.

CPA   Chemical Propulsion Abstracts, mechanized file produced by Chemical Propulsion Information Agency, Applied Physics Laboratory, Johns Hopkins University.

CROSS REFERENCE   Annotation at one place in a document to pertinent information at another place in the document.

CRT   Cathode ray tube, a vacuum tube consisting of an electron gun producing a cathode ray of electrons which impinges on a phosphorescent coating on the back of a viewing screen (for example, a TV screen).

CURRENT AWARENESS SEARCHES   A search of each file update as it is issued, whether weekly, monthly, or quarterly, on a given subject query.

DATA BANK   (See File.)

DATA BASE   (See File.)

DATA CENTER   An organization designed for acquiring, processing, sorting, retrieving, and disseminating data.

DATA FILE   (See File.)

DESCRIPTOR   A word, simple phrase, or number used to identify a concept, idea, or subject.

DEWEY DECIMAL   A numerical system developed by Melvil Dewey for classifying library books and material. Main subject classes and subclasses are designated by three digits and further subdivision is shown by numbers after a decimal point.

DIALIST   Term frequency indexes from the DIALOG files.

DIALOG   Search system used by the Lockheed Online Service.

DIGEST   An informative summary of the contents of a single paper or of several related papers.

DIGITAL COMPUTER   A computer in which the manipulated variables are represented by (binary) digits.

DISK   (See Magnetic Disk.)

DOCUMENT   A record from which information may be derived, such as a book, an engineering drawing, a page from a publication, a tape recording, a journal article, or a government report.

EBCDIC CODE   Extended Binary Coded Decimal Interchange Code, the principal code system used in IBM 360 series computers.

EDGE NOTCHED CARDS   Cards of any size with a series of holes on one or more edges. The holes are used to code information by notching away the edge of the card into the hole. Selection from the deck of cards of those with the desired information is made by inserting a long needle in the pertinent hole position and lifting the deck to allow the notched cards to fall from the needle.

EEDB   ERDA Energy Data Base, produced by the Energy Research and Development Administration.

ELIMINATION FACTOR   The fraction of the total documents in a system not retrieved by a search.

Glossary

ENTRY TERM (OR POINT) The identifying document surrogate used to retrieve a record from a file.

ENVIRON The file, Environmental Information Retrieval Online, produced by the Environmental Protection Agency.

ERIC Educational Resources Information Center, producer of the CIJE data base (Current Index to Journals in Education), and the RIE data base (Resources in Education).

FALSE DROP A reference not pertinent to the subject search which is retrieved by a mechanized system.

FIELD A subdivision of a record containing a category or unit of information.

FILE A group of items of selected accumulated information in machine-readable form prepared for computer searching. Depending on the file format, the item surrogates may be index terms, abstracts, titles, accession numbers, journal references, authors, other information.

FLOW DIAGRAM The sequence of the individual steps of a process, shown in a conventional drawing.

FIXED FIELD The situation in which the field containing the same kind of information is fixed in length and is located in the same relative position in each record.

FORMAT The composition and layout of a printed page such as a computer printout.

FREE TEXT SEARCHING To search the contents of a file by the use of any words or phrases which might be expected to occur in the stored surrogates, whether index terms, title, abstract, whole document, etc.

FUNCTIONAL GROUP Groups of chemical elements such as CH_3 (methyl), C_2H_5 (ethyl), or COOH which are part of the structure of a molecule and display a chemical function.

GEOARCHIVE Machine readable file produced by Geosystems of London, England.

GRID Machine readable file National Geothermal Information Resource, produced by the University of California, Lawrence Berkeley Laboratory.

HARD COPY A document in book, journal, or manuscript form, as opposed to microfilm or magnetic tape.

HASH-CODE Code in which a key, calculated from the input record, is used to address the disk directly rather than by using a directory.

HEADING Main subject heading in a categorized subject index.

HIERARCHIC Arranged or classified in ranks or orders.

HIT A bibliographic citation identified in a file by a search strategy.

HOLDINGS The books, journals, reports, microfiche, etc. constituting a library collection.

IBM CARD An 80 column, 12 row card for keypunching, produced by the International Business Machine Corporation. (See Figs. 2 and 3 in Chap. 6.)

IDENTIFIER In the NTIS subject indexing system, an index term specifically identified as a project name, military nomenclature, identification symbol or number, nickname or jargon, geopolitical name, tradename, or other proper name.

IDIS Machine searchable file Iowa Drug Information Service, produced by the University of Iowa, Iowa Drug Information Service.

INDEX TERM A word or phrase selected as representative of the subject content of a document. Depending on the file specifications, it may be chosen from a controlled vocabulary or it may be any natural language word or phrase.

INFORMATION Facts about any given subject.

INFORMATION BROKER One who contracts to search for and collect information requested by a client.

INFORMATION COUNSELOR One who will counsel and advise as to procedures for obtaining specific information.

INFORMATION RETRIEVAL The recovery of specific information from a collection, file, or group of collections or files. Sometimes limited to the use of the computer to obtain a bibliography of published material on a given subject.

INFORMATION RETRIEVAL CENTER An organization specializing in information retrieval.

INFORMATION SCIENTIST One learned in the science of using, transferring, and communicating facts or data.

INSPEC The machine readable file International Information Services in Physics, Electrotechnology, Computers and Control, produced by the Institution of Electrical Engineers, London.

INTERACTIVE MODE Computer operation making use of an input-output terminal and a program that permits data modification or procedure variation while the operation is going on.

INTERSECTION Documents which have surrogates which will cause them to be retrievals for a specified group of terms (the AND relationship).

INVERTED FILE A file in which documents are listed under each of the terms which are surrogates for the document, rather than being listed in serial order by document number.

ISMEC The machine readable file Information Services in Mechanical Engineering, produced by the Institution of Electrical Engineers, London.

JOURNAL A periodical publication. Frequently an official publication of a scholarly group or organization.

KASC Knowledge Availability Systems Center, University of Pittsburgh. A NASA Industrial Applications Center.

KEYBOARD A bank or row of keys as on a typewriter. Used to keypunch cards or to enter data or commands into a computer.

KEYPUNCH Process of entering codes on cards by use of a keyboard with a punching operation.

Glossary

KEYSORT CARDS   Cards which may be sorted by the key codes punched in them.
KEY TERMS   Words or numbers which represent key elements of a document. May be used as index words.
KEYWORD   (See Key Terms.)
KWIC INDEX   Keyword in context index. A listing, usually of document titles, in which the significant words appear in alphabetical order in a column, with the context immediately preceding and following.
KWOC INDEX   Similar to the KWIC index, but with the significant words appearing as a column followed by as much of the context as the line permits.
LC NUMBERS   Library of Congress Classification. It uses capital letters as notation of the main classes, and integral numbers for subclasses with gaps for future expansion.
LIBRARY OF CONGRESS NUMBERS   (See LC Numbers.)
LIMITING   The act of limiting the portion of the file to be searched, for example by years of publication, journals, languages, or section of abstract journal.
LINK   Code used to indicate associated terms among the index terms of a document.
LOCKHEED   Lockheed Information Systems, a processor of online databases.
LOGICAL OPERATOR   (See Connectors.)
LOGICAL PRODUCTS   (See And.)
LOGICAL SUM   (See Or Relationship.)
MACHINE LANGUAGE   Strings of digits used to give basic instructions to a computer.
MACHINE SEARCHABLE   Information coded so that a computer or sorter can identify the information desired.
MAGNETIC CORE   A ferromagnetic material which can assume either of two magnetic states and thus can be used to store information in a computer.
MAGNETIC DISK   A ferrous oxide platter which stores information in a magnetic form in bands across the platter.
MAGNETIC TAPE   A ribbon of paper, metal, or plastic, coated or impregnated with magnetic material on which information may be stored.
MANAGEMENT INFORMATION   Information of daily use to business management, such as bills outstanding, operations data, and shipments.
MANUAL SEARCHING   To search by hand in hard copy published indexes and journals.
MARGINAL HOLE CARDS   (See Edge Notched Cards.)
MECHANICAL FILE   A file or data bank which can be searched for information by a mechanical device such as a sorter or computer. (See also File.)

MECHANICAL LITERATURE SEARCHING   Using programmed methods to search files of published literature.
MECHANIZED INFORMATION   Information recorded on computer tapes or disks, or on notched cards, so that it may be retrieved by mechanical methods.
MECHANIZED RETRIEVAL   (See Mechanical Literature Searching.)
MEDLARS   MEDLINE preceding 1974, CATLINE, and EPILEPSY; a file produced by the National Library of Medicine.
MEDLINE   The mechanical file MEDLARS Online, produced by the National Library of Medicine.
MESH   Medical Subject Headings Vocabulary File, produced by the National Library of Medicine.
METADEX   The file Metals Abstracts Index, produced by the American Society for Metals.
MICROCARDS   Cards coded for use in a microform information retrieval device. The cards may have inserted one or several pages of microfiche.
MICROFICHE   Photographic sheet film on which is reproduced micro-images of document pages.
MICROFILM   Photographic film on which is recorded graphic information reduced in size.
MICROFORM   A form such as microfiche, microfilm, aperture cards, etc. on which is recorded reduced replicas of information.
MICROGRAPHICS   Minute writing or printing.
MICROPUBLISHING   The field of publishing microforms.
MISSHELVED   Placed on the wrong shelf of a library that is classified in an orderly fashion.
MODEM   A modulation/demodulation device to convert digital signals generated by the computer into an analog form compatible with the telephone lines and back again into digital form.
MONOGRAPH   A single volume dealing with a single subject.
NASA   National Aeronautics and Space Administration.
NC/STRC   North Carolina Science and Technology Research Center, a NASA Industrial Applications Center.
NEEDLE/SORT CARD   Cards which, after notching of hole punches, can be sorted, arranged, and classified by the insertion of a needle. Produced by the Beekley Corporation.
NEGATIVE LOGIC   The use of the NOT connector in Boolean search strategy to eliminate information from the results.
NERAC   New England Research Application Center, a NASA Industrial Application Center.
NESTED PARENTHESES   Representation of the containment within an algebraic expression of another algebraic expression.
NETWORKING   Combining parts or systems to provide a closed information loop.

Glossary

NICEM National Information Center for Educational Media file, produced by the University of Southern California, National Information Center for Educational Media.

NOISE FACTOR The fraction of retrieved documents which are not relevant.

NONBIBLIOGRAPHIC FILE An information file of numeric or graphical data, such as regulatory limits, charts, and maps.

NOTATION OF CONTENT A brief note indicating the contents of the document.

NOT RELATIONSHIP (See <u>Negative Logic.</u>)

NTIS National Technical Information Service.

OFFLINE Peripheral equipment, such as a printer, which may be used as an adjunct to a computer search system without delaying the computer processing.

OMISSION FACTOR The fraction of relevant items in a file which are not retrieved.

ONLINE A continuing, usually two-way, communication hookup between a distant user's terminal and a central searching computer.

ORBIT IV The system developed by System Development Corporation to search files of information online.

OR RELATIONSHIP The Boolean search logic which indicates that any of the terms connected by OR is sufficient to cause a hit.

OVERRIDE FUNCTION A function of a logic relationship which causes it to outweigh any other relationship. The connector NOT is an example.

PAPERCHEM File corresponding to the printed Abstract Bulletin of the Institute of Paper Chemistry, produced by the Institute of Paper Chemistry.

PAPER TAPE Tape made of a continuous ribbon of paper which can be punched in code and used to enter information into, for instance, a teletype machine.

PERMUTED INDEX Rearranging the significant words in a document title or index phrases and making an index in which all the rearrangements are displayed alphabetically.

PERTINENCE FACTOR The fraction of retrieved documents which are relevant.

PIRETS Search system used by the University of Pittsburgh.

POSTINGS DICTIONARY A dictionary of index terms giving the number of document entries in the file posted to each term.

POSTINGS The number of documents entered per term in a file.

PRECISION The fraction of retrieved documents which are relevant.

PRINTOUT The results of a search which are printed out by offline or online auxilliary units to the computer, in the format requested.

PROGRAM Instructions keyed into the computer which cause it to perform tasks by a given sequence of operations.

PROJECT PROFILE   The evaluated, classified bibliography presented to the client as a result of a search. As developed by KASC, it gives the background of the search.
PROMT   Computer searchable file Predicasts Market Abstracts, produced by Predicasts, Inc.
PUNCHED CARDS   (See IBM Card and Edge Notched Cards.)
RECALL   The fraction of relevant documents retrieved.
RANDOM ACCESS DISKS   Disks on which information is coded so that any item may be found without searching through other items.
RECORD   Collection of related surrogates or data elements, words, or codes which can logically be considered as associated with a single bibliographic item in a file.
RECORDAK   Programmed film viewer which permits selection of pages to be viewed on an optical screen. Product of Eastman Kodak.
REFERENCE   Instruction telling where to find specific information such as a document.
REFERENCE BOOK   A book intended to be a source of information such as data, procedures, or history.
REGISTRY NUMBER   A 5 digits-2 digits-1 digit number issued by Chemical Abstracts Service to give a permanent, unique, computer-checkable identification to every chemical substance within the CAS data base.
REPORT   A document containing the results of an investigation, which may be a literature search.
RESOLUTION FACTOR   The fraction of documents in a file that are retrieved.
RETRIEVAL SERVICE CENTER   A center specializing in the retrieval of published literature.
RETROSPECTIVE SEARCH   A search of the back issues of a computerized file, or of hard-copy indexes of an abstract journal.
REVIEW   A critical evaluation of a document. (See also State-of-the-Art Report.)
RIC   Computerized file Rare Earth Information Center, produced by Iowa State University, Institute for Atomic Research, and Ames Laboratory.
ROLE   A device such as a character, code, or syntax used to indicate the relationships between terms used in indexing.
SCISEARCH   The computerized Science Citation Index, produced by the Institute for Scientific Information.
SDC   System Development Corporation, an online bibliographic retrieval processor.
SDI   Selective dissemination of information. The provision at regular intervals of references, abstracts, or documents to users in specific subject areas requested.
SEARCH STRATEGY   The array of terms (and the relationships between them) that is entered into a computer for the purpose of making a search.
SHE   Subject Headings for Engineering, published by Engineering Index Inc.

Glossary

SMART System devised by G. Salton for retrieving information from computer memory.
SOCSEARCH Computerized file of the social and behavioral sciences portion of the Citation Index, produced by the Institute for Scientific Information.
SORTER Mechanical device for the sorting of keypunched cards.
SSIE The file Smithsonian Science Information Exchange, produced by Smithsonian Science Information Exchange, Inc.
STAIRS A system for retrieving information from computer memory, used by the International Business Machine Corporation.
STATE-OF-THE-ART REPORT A complete, up-to-date, critical report about information available on a specific problem or subject.
STEM WORD (See Word Stem.)
STOP WORD A word, such as "the," "a," or "by," not included in the coding of the item terms into a computer searchable file.
STRATEGY (See Search Strategy.)
STRING SEARCH Strings of terms, with or without connectors, which may be searched as phrases or sentences.
STRUCTURAL FRAGMENT (See Functional Group.)
STRUCTURED BIBLIOGRAPHY A bibliography structured by subject and/or subject subheading, or by corporate source origin, or in some other pattern.
SUBFILE A subdivision of a file.
SUBHEADING A heading indicating a subdivision of the subject of a main heading.
SUBROUTINE A set of instructions directing a computer to carry out a well-defined mathematical or logical operation. A subunit of a routine, usually coded so that it can be introduced as a prepackaged method of achieving the desired result.
SUBSET A set contained within a set.
SURROGATE A term which can be manipulated as a substitute for a document. It can be a number, an index term, an author, a journal page, etc.
TAPE (See Magnetic Tape and Paper Tape.)
TELENET Data communications network service operating over dial-in telephone lines.
TERMINAL A computer unit which is used for both input and output. It can be used interactively and may be connected to the computer by hardline or by telecommunications linkage.
TERM A word, phrase, symbol, number, or code descriptive of a document.
THESAURUS A pre- or postcontrolled list of descriptors for a specified subject field. It will contain cross references to synonyms, and scope notes.
THREE-WAY INTERSECTION Documents which will be identified by a group of three terms. (See Intersection.)

THRESHOLD WEIGHT   In a strategy operating on the basis of weighted terms, the total weight above which a document will be identified as relevant.

TRUNCATION   Removing a portion of a word so that the remainder can be used as a search term to identify all words containing the word stem.

TWO-WAY INTERSECTION   Documents which will be identified by a group of two terms. (See <u>Intersection</u>.)

TYMNET   Data communications network operating over dial-in telephone lines.

VENN DIAGRAM   Diagrammatic approach to the presentation of relationships among classes. Intersections of closed areas representing classes indicate areas of common application of the intersecting classes. The scheme was developed by John Venn.

WAA   The computerized file World Aluminum Abstracts, produced by the American Society for Metals.

WEIGHTED TERM   In a search system using weights, the terms for which weights have been assigned. (See <u>Threshold Weight</u>.)

WEIGHTING   Search system in which the various terms are assigned various weights and a document is retrieved when the threshold weight results from the summing of the weights of the terms associated with the document. (See <u>Threshold Weight</u>.)

WESRAC   Western Research Application Center. One of the NASA Industrial Applications Centers.

WISWESSER LINE NOTATION   The Wiswesser Line-Formula Notation is a method of describing the molecular structure of a chemical in a single line of print. Letters are used to denote functional groups, numbers to express length of alkyl chains and sizes of rings.

WORD STEM   A word stem or word root is a portion of a word which can be used to retrieve a number of words containing that stem or root.

Index

A

ABI INFORM, 25, 26
Abstract Number, 114, 121 (see also Accession number)
Abstracts, 32, 69, 80, 83, 100, 112-114, 116, 119
Accession number, (see also Abstract Number) 52, 111, 114, 116, 118, 119
Access point, 31
ADJ, 39
Allcock, Harry M., 30
Alloy Data Center, 122
Alphanumerics, 31, 32, 119
American National Standards Institute, 113
American Society for Metals, 67
AND Connector (Operator), 53, 102, 118, 120
Aperture cards, 1, 83, 111
APILIT, 22, 24
Arnett, Edward M., 30
Articles, 6
ASCII Code, 113
ASIS, 17
Authorities, 5
Authors, 99, 100, 113, 114, 116, 118
 affiliations, 42, 69, 113, 116
 field, 40, 41, 112
Automated profile, 62
Automated search, 13
Automatic strategy, 62
Automatic truncation, 113

B

Background information (see State-of-the-art)
Bandwagon, jump on the, 98
Barker, F. H., 105
Baser, K. H., 90
Batch processing, 100, 112, 117, 120
Battelle Memorial Institute, 9
BCD code, 21
Becker, Joseph, 67, 123
Belzer, Jack, 123
Bibliography, 68, 72, 74
 with abstracts, 68, 80, 111
 annotated, 68, 80
 categorized, 80, 84
 closeness of fit, 74
 edited, 79, 81
 evaluated, 8
 number of journals covered, 74
 purpose, 74, 79
 size, 74, 107
 structured, 68, 80, 81
 time span, 74
Biblio-Profile, 81, 82
Binary code, 112, 113
BIOSIS, 13, 22, 24, 66
Bit, 21, 111, 113
Books, 117
Boolean logic, 52, 60, 120, 121
Boole, George, 67
Bowman, Walker H., 30
Broad strategy, 62, 96, 98. 99

Broad, William J., 30
Brokers, 121, 122
Browsing, 99
BRS, 22, 122
Bubble memory, 107, 111
Burchinal, Lee G., 124
Burroughs, Barbara E., 124
Byrne, Jerry R., 66
Byte, 21

C

CACON, 13, 14, 16, 18, 22, 24, 100, 117
Card
 catalogs, 6, 33
 decks, 112
 index (see Card, catalogs)
 reader, 107
 sorter, 107
Carroll, John M., 67
Cartridges, 83, 111
Caruso, Elaine, 124
CASCIA, 33
CA Selects, 9
Catalogs, 6, 115
Categorization, 115
CBCC Code 22, 47
Chemical Abstracts, 7, 8, 34, 35, 50, 66, 90, 99, 111, 113
 file (see CACON)
 section, 50, 99, 117
 volume indexes, 70
Chronological serial order, 114
Citation
 bibliographic, 69, 74, 114
 index, 72
Cited reference, 72, 113
Cleveland, Donald B., 66
Closed coordinated index, 98
Closed indexing, 55, 99
Closeness of fit, 77
CODEN, 18, 43, 45, 112
Codes, 1, 20, 31, 112, 117, 119
 See also ASCII code, EBCDIC code, Digital codes, Fixed length numeric codes, Hash code

Cohen, S. M., 90
Command language, 118
Communication network, 8, 111, 122
COMPENDEX, 13, 17, 18, 20-22, 24, 36, 56
Computer
 analog, 106
 core, 111 (see also Core memory)
 digital, 106
 instructions, 106
 manipulation, 106
 memory, 106, 111, 118
 printout (see Printout)
 processing, 1, 121
 programs, 8, 118
 storage, 106, 117, 120
 terminal, 8, 122
CONDENSATES (see CACON)
Connectivity tables, 47
Connectors
 See also AND, NOT, OR, 121
Controlled indexing, 120
Controlled vocabulary, 119
Coordinated index, 32, 36
Copyright restrictions, 123
Core memory
 See also Computer core, 2, 107, 111
Corporate source, 42
Corrosion, 14
Costs, 74, 92, 98-100, 107, 117, 120
CPA, 23, 25
CRC Handbook of Chemistry and Physics, 94
Cross reference, 119
CRT, 72, 111
Cuadro, Carlos A., 12
Current awareness searches, 102-104

D

Data bank (see Data bases)
Data base elements, 116
 printable, 20, 21

Index

[Data base elements (cont'd.)]
  searchable, 20, 21, 31, 112, 113
Data bases, 15, 83
  combination, 120, 121
  nonbibliographic, 8, 13, 43
Data centers, 121, 122
Data files (see Data bases)
Data management systems, 119
Data storage, 111
Data tables, 72
Davis, H. D., 124
Dayton, David L., 66, 90
Dennis, D. E., 67
Descriptor, 32, 69, 114
Dewey decimal numbers, 6
Diagrams (see Graphs)
DIALIST, 36, 39, 117
DIALOG, 119-121
Dictionaries, 119
Digest, 68, 82, 88
Digital codes, 43, 112
Direct access, 116
Directories, 15, 112
Directory of Computer Readable Data Bases, 17
Disks (see Magnetic disks)
Documents, 20, 72, 74, 80, 83, 98, 102, 111, 113
Double-word term, 32
Dow-Jones News/Retrieval, 8, 122
Drake, Miriam A., 124
Duplicate papers (see Repetitive publishing)
Duplicate references, 120
Duplicate tapes, 112

E

EBCDIC code, 21, 113
Edge notched cards, 83, 107, 118
Edited results, 68, 77, 79, 81
Editing, manual, 77
Editorial selection, 18
EEDB, 22, 23
Electrical engineering, 13
Electrical properties alloys, 100
Electronic access, 117
Electron microscopy, 74
El Hadidy, Bahaa, 124
Elimination factor, 92
Elman, Stanley A., 105
Energy, 62
ENGINEERING INDEX, 7, 8, 55, 67, 99, 100, 124
Engineers Joint Council, 67
Entry term (or point), 31, 51, 113
ENVIRON, 22, 23
Environmental control, 62
ERIC, 22, 24
Error free punched tape, 111
Error message, 113
Expressing the information need, 3

F

Fact retrieval, 94, 118
Falk Library of Medicine, University of Pittsburgh, 22
False drop, 62, 68, 77, 116
Farmer, Nick A., 67
Fayen, E. G., 67
Feedback modification, 120, 121
Fields, 112, 113
Files
  academic, 23
  back, 117
  bibliographic, 13, 111, 113, 114, 119
  card, 69, 107
  characteristics, 31
  commercially produced, 25
  coverage, 20, 100
  dictionary, 36
  discipline tailored, 62
  government, 22
  headings, 51
  indexed, 117
  in-house, 117
  items, 114
  organization, 114
  personal, 107
  produced by professional organizations, 22
  restricted, 113

[Files (cont'd.)]
  sequential, 117
  size, 16
  special, 83
  time span, 20
Film, 83, 107, 111
Film reader, 1
Fixed field, 113
Fixed length numeric codes, 117
Flanagan, Carolyn, 29
Flow diagram, 31, 102, 104
Format, 31
Free text, 32, 36, 40, 98, 99, 116, 119, 120
Functional group (see Structure, chemical; Structure, molecular)

G

Galvin, Thomas J., 124
Garfield, E., 67, 90
General Electric Company, 122
Generic index, 70, 98, 102, 120
Generic term, 119
Gould, Jay R., 90
Government files, 121
Granito, C. E., 67
Graphs, 72, 83, 119
Greater than, 120, 121
GRID, 23, 25

H

Hard copy abstract journal, 80, 102
Hash code, 117, 118
Hawkins, Donald T., 30, 66
Hayes, R. M., 67, 123
Heading, 32
Heading-subheading entry, 33, 119
Hirst, Graeme, 30
Hit, 53, 59
Hoegberg, Erick I., 30
Holdings, 122
Holm, Bart E., 30
Howell, Mary Gertrude, 30

Huber, M. L., 67
Hyslop, Marjorie R., 30

I

IBM card, 69, 107, 109, 110
Identification number, 122
Identifier, 32
IDIS, 25
Illinois Institute of Technology Research Institute, 8
Image page, 111
Indexes, 70, 115
  chemical substance, 33
  permuted, 47
Indexing, 98
  depth, 18, 33
  inaccuracies, 103
  limited, 55
  nongeneric, 102
Index term, 69, 113, 114, 116
  acceptable, 32, 36, 57, 112, 113, 116, 119
  merged, 39
Information
  broker, 68
  business, 18
  consultant, 68
  counselor, 68
  explosion, 13
  liaison, 68
  mechanically retrieved, 8
  needs, 3
  retrieval center, 8
  scientists, 68, 77, 100
  sources of, 1
  stored, 8, 107
  systems, internal, 8
  technical, 7
Information Center for Hearing, Speech and Disorders of Human Communication, Johns Hopkins, 81
INSPEC, 13, 22, 24, 100

Institute for Scientific Information, Inc., 8, 25, 26, 73, 122
Interactive mode (see Online)
Internal stem search, 43
Intersection, 53
  See also Logical product; AND connector
Inverted file, 115-118
ISMEC, 28
Item number (see Accession number; Abstract number)
Iteration, 100, 114

J

Johnson, Simon S., 90
Johns, Trisha M., 30
Jones, A. C., 11
Journal Citation Reports, 18
Journals
  abstract, 7, 102
  core, 18, 99
  coverage, 19, 100, 117
  information science, 9
  names and dates, 42, 69
  storage, 111
  technical, 7
  titles, 40, 113, 114, 116

K

KASC, University of Pittsburgh, 22, 81, 121
Kellog, Charles H., 124
Kennedy, H. E., 29
Kent, Allen, 30, 67, 105, 123, 124
Keyboard punching, 111
Keying, 111
Keypunched cards, 107, 111, 112
Keysort cards, 107
Key terms (see Keywords)
Keywords, 4, 5, 31, 32, 40, 50, 113, 121
Kilgour, F. G., 124
Kobe, Kenneth Albert, 91

Kolb, Margaret C., 91, 123
Krathwohl, David R., 90
Kuney, Joseph H., 30
KWIC index, 47, 70
KWOC index, 70, 71

L

Lancaster, F. W., 67, 105
Language, 69, 77, 99, 113, 114
Less than, 120, 121
Libraries, 1, 121, 122
Library of Congress, 13, 29
Library of Congress numbers, 6
Limiting, 52, 92, 99, 118, 120, 121
Links, 52
Literature
  collections, 93
  survey, 82, 89
Lockheed-DIALOG subject guide, 17
Lockheed Missiles and Space Co., 8, 15, 21, 22, 29, 66, 100, 101, 106, 122, 124
Logical operator, 52
Logical product, 53, 55, 56
Logical sum, 53, 55, 56
Longman, Janet S., 67
Long-term memory, 112
Look-up, 3
Lotz, John W., 30
Low precision, 94
Luke, Ann W., 12
Lunin, Lois F., 90

M

Machine readable, 83
Machine searchable, 20
Magnetic core (see Computer core)
Magnetic disks, 1, 2, 8, 107, 111, 112, 116, 121
Magnetic tapes, 1, 2, 8, 69, 107, 111, 112, 116, 121, 123
Major headings, 99
Management information, 83

Manheimer, M. L., 90
Manual preparation, 3, 100
Marcus, Martin J., 30
Marginal hole cards, 107
Martin, James, 91
Match (see Hit)
MCIC, Metals and Ceramic Information Center, 9
Mead Data Central, 8
Meadow, Charles T., 123
Mechanical Files (see Files)
Mechanical literature search (see Automated search)
Mechanized retrieval (see Automated search)
MEDLARS, 22, 23, 36
MEDLINE, 22, 23, 36
Melting point, 94
Memory devices, 8
MESH, 36, 37
METADEX, 13, 14, 16-18, 22, 24, 100
Microcards, 111
Microfiche, 33, 72, 83, 111
Microfilm, 1, 111
Microform, 83
Microimages, 111
Microphotography, 111
Minker, Jack, 67
Monographs, 6, 117
Mount, Ellis, 66

N

Narrow strategy, 62, 96, 98
NASA, 12, 14, 22, 23, 66, 67
NASA Industrial Application Centers, 8, 121
NASA Technology Utilization Office, 124
NASA thesaurus, 36, 38, 66
National Bureau of Standards, 122
Natural phenomena, 98
Needle/sort, 107, 108, 118
Negation, 60
  See also Negative logic

Negative logic, 53, 54, 60
Neperud, R., 124
NERAC, 121
Nested parentheses, 54, 120, 121
Networking, 121, 122, 123
Newman, Pauline, 19
Newspaper articles, 72, 113
New York Times Information Bank, 8, 25, 26, 43, 46, 72, 117
NICEM, 23, 25
Nine fill, 119
Noise factor, 93
Nonrelevant citations (see False drops)
Norgaard, Margaret, 90
Notation of content, 32
Notched cards, 62, 107, 111
Nothing has been published, 94
NOT relationship, 118, 120
NTIS, 22, 23, 31
Number limit, 74
Numerical data, 43, 72, 113, 114, 119, 122
Numeric codes, 43

O

Offline printout, 8, 106
O'Leary, Patrick T., 30
Omission factor, 93
Online, 8, 54, 62, 72, 99-101, 106, 112, 117, 120, 121
Online services, 121, 122
Online, the magazine, 18
Oppenheim, Charles, 29
Optically sensible dots, 111
ORBIT, 119-121
OR connector (operator), 53, 102, 118, 120
Organizations selling mechanical searches, 121
Output
  forms, 83
  size, 99
Overlap, 13, 14, 117
Override function, 54, 60

Index

P

PAPERCHEM, 17
Paper tape, 111
Parity bit, 113
Park, Margaret K., 67
Patent literature, 17
Patent searching, 20
Peak publication year, 76, 77, 98, 99
Peltola, Eero, 67
Perry, J. W., 105
Pertinence factor, 92
Peters, Paul E., 124
Petrarca, E., 67
Petroleum Abstracts, 23, 25
Photocopies, 102
Phrases (see String search)
Pilch, Wolfgang, 30
PIRETS, 39, 66, 119-121
Postings, 36, 53, 60, 120, 121
Postings dictionary, 36, 47, 61
Precision, 62, 93-99
PREDICASTS, 25, 26, 51, 73, 90
Primary memory (see Core memory)
Printout, 68, 69, 79, 83, 120
Prints, 72
Problem solving, 3
Process metallurgy, 18
Products of mechanized retrieval, 69
Professional salaries, 100
Profile, 102
Program
  print, 68, 92
  search, 20, 92, 106
Project profile, 81
PROMT, 72
Publication abbreviations, 46
  See also CODEN
Publication dates, 52, 99, 118
Punched cards, 107, 111, 118
Purdue University, 122

R

Radwin, Mark S., 124
Random access disks, 112
Random coding, 107
Ranking, 52, 120, 121
Raw computer output, 68, 80, 92
Reading machine, 83
Recall, 62, 93, 96-99
Record
  bibliographic, 112, 113
  format, 21, 83, 112, 113, 118
Recordak, 83, 111
Red herring, 33
Reference books, 6, 58, 100, 102, 117, 118
Reference list (see Bibliography)
References (see Bibliographic citations)
Registry number, 43, 114
Related terms, 117
Relaxed strategy, 57, 58
Relevant items (documents), 55, 80, 93-96, 98, 99
Repetitive publishing, 2
Reports, 6, 68, 82, 83, 89
Resolution factor, 92
Retrieval services
  bibliographic, 8
  centers, 121
Retrospective search, 102, 117
Reverse chronological order, 77
Review, 68, 82
RIC, 23, 25
Rivers, William L., 90
Robson, Alan, 67
Roles, 52
Rolling mill design, 100
Rouse, Sandra H., 29
Rush, James E., 30
Ryno, Dorothy I., 30

S

Salton, G., 123, 124
SCAN, 9
Schenk, H. R., 66
Schermer, Carole A., 67
Schipma, Peter B., 124

Science Abstracts, 7
Scientific and Technical Aerospace
 Reports, 7
SCISEARCH, 73
SDC, 21, 106, 122, 124
SDI (see Current awareness
 searches)
Search
 effectiveness, 92, 93
 efficiency, 62, 94-96
 failed, 95, 102
 general, 98
 generically, 50, 98 (see also
  hierarchic)
 goal, 92
 hierarchic, 119, 120
 incomplete, 94, 97
 instructions, 20
 manual, 76, 94, 100, 102
 pattern, 114
 preparation, 100
 procedures, 64, 106, 118
 product, 72, 106
 program, capabilities of, 31, 32
 requests, 92
 statement, 5
 strategy, 31
 subject, 40, 113
 substructure, 50
 unbalanced, 95
 words (terms), 100, 121
 work flow, 63
Secondary journal, 76
Semiconductor memory, 107
Sets, 55
Sharp, Geoffrey, 30
SHE, 51, 117
Sherman, Theodore A., 90
SIC, 51
Skaff, Joey, 124
SMART, 119, 121
Smith, E. G., 66
Sociological Abstracts, 7
Sommar, H. G., 67
Sorting, 60, 62, 118

SSIE, 22, 24
STAIRS, 119, 121
State-of-the-art, 3, 77, 82
State University of New York, 122
Stem-word (see Word stem)
Stop-word, 40
Storage (see Computer storage)
Strategy, 50, 54, 56-62, 77, 95-100,
 102
 modifiers, 99, 111, 112, 120-123
STRC, 122
String search, 39, 40, 118, 120
Structure
 chemical, 43, 114
 fragment, 50
 molecular, 47
Strunk, William Jr., 90
Subfile, 94, 116
Subheading, 32, 119
Subject
 breadth, 74
 fields, 17
 terms (words), 31, 32, 98
Subroutine, 120
Subset, 113, 117
Summaries, 6
Superconductive Materials Data
 Center, 122
Surrogate (see Data base elements)
Sutherland, Elspeth A., 29
Sweet, Richard, 90
Synonyms, 55, 95
System capabilities, 96
System Development Corporation, 8,
 15
 See also SDC

T

Tabular reports, 83, 119
Tague, Jean M., 67
Tape
 library, 112, 117
 specifications, 21
 See also Magnetic tapes
Teitlebaum, Henry H., 30

TELENET, 122
Teletype machines, 111
Temporary memory, 112
Teplitz, A., 124
Terminology, 4
Textbook, 6
Thermophysical Properties Center, 122
Thesauri, 20, 36, 58, 102
Three letter stems, 50
Three-way intersection, 55, 56, 102
Threshold weight, 59
Tichy, H. J., 91
Tight strategy (see Narrow strategy)
Time lag, 76
Time span, 74, 98, 99
Time to examine results, 99
Titanium, 14, 100
Title words (terms), 32, 40, 57, 69, 98, 113, 114, 116, 119
Translating services, 77
Tree structure, 36, 37
Truncation, 31, 43, 47, 118, 121
Two-way intersection (see Two-way subject search)
Two-way subject search, 77, 102
TYMNET, 122

U

Ulman, Joseph N. Jr., 90
Ultrafiche, 111
University of Connecticut, 122
University of Georgia Information Center, 8, 122
University of Illinois, 122
University of North Carolina, 122
University of Pittsburgh, 121, 124
University of Southern California, 122

Unsatisfactory results, 102
User aids, 20
User reactions, 92, 102

V

Valicenti, Aldona K., 30
Variable field length, 113
Veal, D. C., 105
Venn diagram, 53
Viewer, 111
  See also Recordak; CRT
Vocabulary lists, 20

W

WAA, 13, 16, 17
Watkins, P. B., 90
Wegmuller, F., 66
Weighted term (see Weighting)
Weighting, 52, 59, 60, 121
Wente, V. A., 12
WESRAC, 122
Western Reserve University, 92
White, E. B., 90
Wicker, R., 124
Wigington, Ronald L., 67
Williams, B. J. S., 123
Williams, Martha E., 29
Wilson, Gerald A., 67
Wiswesser line notation, 47, 114
Woodburn, Henry M., 30
Wood, James L., 29
Wooldridge, Susan, 91
Word stem, 43, 120
Wratscho, Werner, 30
Wyatt, B. K., 105

Y

Young, G. A., 12